W9-BDB-551

101 Mac Tips

Safari & OS X

**Tips,Tricks and Techniques
To Help You Get
the Most From Your Mac**

by Gary Rosenzweig

First Edition, February 2016

Table of Contents

Introduction and Notes

This book is intended to be a quick, fun journey of discovery. If you are like me, you get a little bit of pleasure from finding a cool hidden or obscure feature on your Mac. If this feature helps you do things faster or more efficiently, then all the better.

I've written this book to share some of my favorite Mac tips. Many of these I use several times each day. Yet I find that when I talk to other Mac users, they don't even know about some of them. Likewise, I find new tips almost every week. You never stop learning.

The best way to learn a new tip is to try it out for yourself. It is very unlikely that you'll need a tip at the exact moment you read about it. Trying it out so you store it away in your memory is a good idea. Then when you need it, you know it.

The tips in this book all work on Macs running OS X 10.11, also known as El Capitan. Most of them worked on versions before that, and I'm sure most of them will continue to work on OS X 10.12 and forward.

What This Book Covers

Everyone uses their Mac in a different way. Some people may rarely use anything but Safari to browse the web. Others may use dozens of different apps to do research, develop websites, or maintain a business. A graphic artist may use Photoshop all day long and rarely surf the web or check email.

I set the scope of this book to just the operating system itself, OS X, and Safari – the primary web browser used by most Mac users – so you'll find lots of tips about working with files, setting System Preferences, and viewing websites. This forms the foundation experience for almost all Mac users.

I stayed away from other apps, like Mail, Messages, Contacts, Reminders, Calendar, and so on. Surely another 101 tips could come from just those alone. Then there are apps like Pages, Numbers, Keynote, iMovie, and so on. There's another 101.

But I didn't want this book to become too unwieldy or expensive. So I'll focus on OS X and Safari here and perhaps cover tips for those other apps, or use a more comprehensive approach for them, in a future book or video series.

Bonus Materials

In addition to the 101 tips here, I've put together a few more just-for-fun ones. These are crazy easter eggs hidden in your Mac and other fun stuff. In addition, any notes, updates or errata for this book will be found there. I may add some demonstration videos there, too, if I get enough requests about a particular tip.

To get to the bonus materials section, just go to **http://macmost.com/tips-book-bonus** and register your book. All you need is your email address and a secret code that is included on the last page of this book. Enter that and you'll get free access.

About the Author

Gary Rosenzweig is the host and producer of MacMost.com, a website dedicated to helping people get the most from their Macs and other Apple products. Gary has been writing about computers and technology for 20 years. His books include the best-selling *My iPad* series (2010-present) and the *MacMost Guide to Switching to the Mac* (2009). He has created more than 1,000 free video tutorials for MacMost.com. He also creates iOS and web-based games and apps.

Gary's first computer was a TRS-80 Model III in 1982. His first Apple product was an Apple IIe in 1986. He has a bachelor's degree in computer science from Drexel University and a master's degree in journalism from the University of North Carolina.

You can follow Gary at **MacMost.com**, on Twitter **@rosenz** and on Facebook at **http://facebook.com/macmost**. You can email him at **questions@macmost.com**.

For free video tutorials about how to get the most from your Mac, plus tips, a weekly newsletter and a Q&A forum, visit:

http://macmost.com

Section 1 — Getting Started

1. Accessing Context Menus

You will notice that a lot of these tips involve using context menus. These are menus you get when you **control+click** on an object. For instance, if you **control+click** on a file in the Finder, you get a context menu that looks like this.

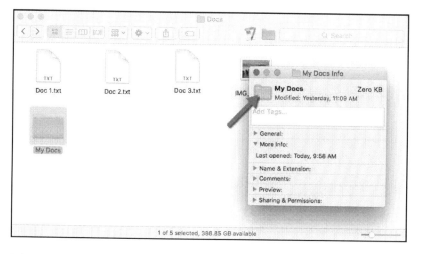

There are many ways to access these context menus. Using a **control+click** is just one, and it is the one that almost always works, no matter which other preferences you have set or which input devices you are using.

All modern Macs come with a multi-button mouse, however. By default, clicking the secondary button, usually the right side of your mouse, will bring up the context menu. Go to **System Preferences**, **Mouse** to configure the secondary button, or set another mouse action to bring up the context menu.

Likewise, if you use a trackpad on a MacBook, or Apple's desktop trackpad, then the Trackpad settings in System

Preferences will allow you to configure a **Secondary click**. By default, it is set to **Click or tap with two fingers**.

Learning to use context menus is very important if you want to use your Mac quickly and efficiently. Just about any object in any app can be **control+clicked** to bring up the context menu with functions that pertain to that object. Try it in Pages, Numbers, Keynote, Mail, Safari, Photos, and everywhere.

You can even use context menus on nothing. Try **control+click** on the background of the Desktop, or on a Finder window. Try **control+click** on a blank space in a web page in Safari. If there is some aspect of an app or the operating system that has options, chances are **control+click** will bring up a context menu.

2. Print Anything As a PDF

PDF stands for portable document format. It is a document, usually text and images, that should look exactly the same whether viewed on a Mac, PC, tablet, phone or anywhere. It is kind of the digital equivalent of paper. Electronic books often come in PDF format, as do documents, corporate memos, government forms, and so on.

If you want to save something you are looking at on your Mac, you may be tempted to print it out. But instead of wasting the paper, you can use this technique to "print as PDF." This creates a file that can be opened in the Preview app on your Mac as well as a variety of other apps on your Mac, iOS devices, Windows computers, and so on. You can also email or share a PDF file any way you would share any type of file. So they are handy.

You can create a PDF from almost anything. If you can print it from your Mac, you can create a PDF.

To do this, start as if you are going to print. Usually this means choosing **File**, **Print**. This should bring up the Print dialog. It will look different depending on which app you are using. But in most cases, you will see the **PDF** button at the bottom left.

Click that button and then choose **Save As PDF**. This will then prompt you for a location and filename, as if you were saving a document in any application. The result will be a PDF file.

I use this when I get to the last page on a website after ordering a product. Usually, there will be a confirmation page and the instructions "Please print this page." I print it as a PDF instead of wasting the paper.

Note that you can always change your mind and open the PDF in the Preview app to print it later. I'll do this for airplane boarding passes. I'll print to a PDF, and then later, I will open the PDF in Preview and print it before leaving for the airport.

You can also use this in apps that don't provide any other way to export a PDF. For instance, if you are working in a business app and want to share a report with someone via email, you can use **File**, **Print**, **Save as PDF**, and then email that PDF. As a matter of fact, further down the menu after **Save as PDF,** you will find a **Mail PDF** function that will save you some steps.

Another option you get when you press the **PDF** button is to **Open PDF in Preview**. This will create a PDF, open it in Preview, but not save it. You can then choose to save, print, or just look at it. I use this when I think I want to save a web page from Safari, but I want to check to see what it will look like as a PDF first. Many websites have special code that makes them look considerably different when printed.

3. Taking Screen Shots

There are various reasons why you may want to capture what you see on the screen. And there are various ways to do this, including lots of third-party software. But for basic screen shots, you can just use the system functions.

By default there are four different keyboard shortcuts for taking screen shots. Because these are customizable, you should check in System Preferences under **Keyboard, Shortcuts** and look for the **Screen Shots** category. If yours have been set to something different, you can always change them back, or to something else.

shift+command+3	Save the whole screen
control+shift+command+3	Copy the screen to the clipboard
shift+command+4	Save a selected area
control+shift+command+4	Copy a selected area to the clipboard

The clipboard functions are generally more useful as you can paste directly into an email, Pages document, or another app. You can even launch Preview, then choose **File**, **New from Clipboard** to quickly create a document from the screen shot. Then you can even use Preview to annotate it before saving it.

If you use the two functions that allow you to select an area, then you get a cross-hairs cursor and can drag a rectangle around an area of the screen to capture that area. You even see the exact pixel size of the area as you drag.

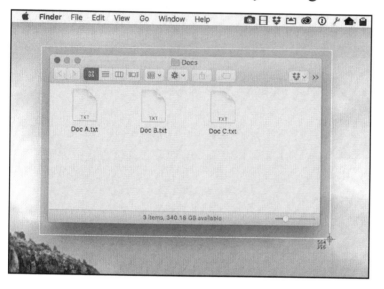

While you are dragging, you can press the spacebar and you get a camera cursor. Now you can move the mouse over any window and capture that window.

If you want even more screen shot functions without going to a third-party app, look for the Grab app in your Applications/ Utilities folder. With Grab, you can set up a timed screen shot. A timed screen shot is captured after a delay of a few seconds. This way you can select menu items and show things that you couldn't if you had to use the standard screen shot keyboard shortcuts.

Section 2 — Using Apps

4. Find An App To Open a Document

So say you get a document from a colleague. You double-click it, but it turns out you don't have an app that will open that type of document. You could search around for such an app, but there is a quicker way to find one.

Control+click on the app, and from the context menu select **Open With**. Look at the bottom of the list and you'll see **App Store...** Select that and it will open the Mac App Store and list any apps that claim to be able to deal with that file.

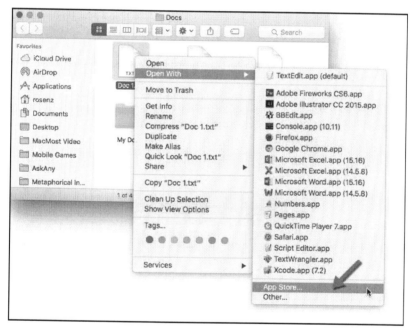

You can also start in the App Store app and use the search box to find apps that claim to handle files with a specific extension. For instance, you could type "extension:doc" in the search box to see apps that handle Word documents.

5. Force Quit Apps

Sometimes apps misbehave. If an app freezes on you, then the first thing you should try to do is to quit gracefully by selecting the application in the menu and choosing **Quit**. But if you can't, then it is time to force quit.

Using **command+option+esc** will bring up the Force Quit Applications window with a list of apps that are currently running. You can select the app and then try the **Force Quit** button.

You can skip the window by using the Apple menu and the **Force Quit...** menu item. It will also bring up the Force Quit Applications window. But if you hold down the **shift** key, or just use the full **shift+command+option+esc** shortcut, it will immediately force-quit the current application.

If you ever get desperate because an app won't even force-quit, then try restarting. If even that doesn't work, try running an app on your Mac named Activity Monitor. Look for the app by name in the list and select it. Then click the stop-sign-shaped x button at the top left.

6. Customize Toolbars

The Finder, Mail, Safari, Pages, and almost all Apple-created apps will allow you to customize the document window toolbar. You can get rid of items you don't use, and add easy access to other functions.

To customize the toolbar, look for **View**, **Customize Toolbar...** in the menu bar. Or **control+click** on the toolbar and choose **Customize Toolbar**.

From this special set of controls, you can drag a button onto the toolbar, or drag it down off of it. You can also re-arrange the items by dragging them left and right in the toolbar. There is even a space and a flexible space that you can add to help you group toolbar items.

The best way to get the most from customizing the toolbar is to play around with it. Try adding things and removing things, rearranging them and adding spaces. Then drag the default set to the toolbar to erase your work and start again.

If you find yourself often using a hard-to-get-to function in an app, see if you can customize the toolbar to make that function easy to access.

You can also use the **Show** option at the bottom of this control to choose to view icons, text or both.

7. Use the Application Switcher

Efficient Mac users rarely use the Dock or the Finder to switch between apps. Instead, they use the Application Switcher. All you need to do is press **command+tab** to switch between your current app and the last app.

However, if you hold down **command**, then press **tab** and release it while still holding down **command**, the Application Switcher appears. Now, while still holding **command** down, you can tap the **tab** key to move the highlight from one app to another, through your entire list of open apps.

When you release the **command** key, you'll jump to that app.

You can also use the mouse when you have the Application Switcher on the screen. With the command key still down, you can click an app to jump to it. You can also use **shift+tab** to move backward through the list, though note that if you continue to **tab**, you'll loop from the last item back to the first.

8. Add An Application Launcher To Your Dock

Your Dock is already an app launcher, of course. It can get crowded if you add a lot of apps. But there is a way to add a single item that gives you access to every single app on your Mac.

To do this, first go in the Finder to one level above your Applications folder. You can do this by using **Go, Computer**. Then double-click to enter your hard drive. At the top level of your hard drive, you'll see the Applications folder. Now drag that to the right side of the Dock. It must be the right side, to the right of the vertical dividing line.

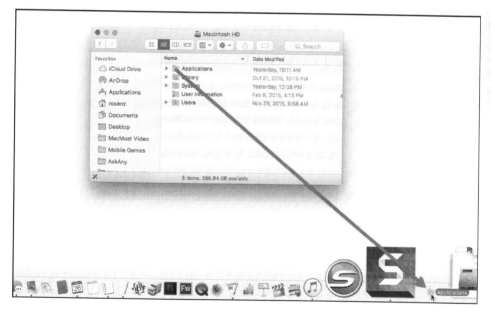

Next, **control+click** on the resulting new icon in your Dock. Then select **List** under **View content as** and **Folder** under **Display as**.

Now when you click on this Dock icon, you'll see a long list of apps and can select any one to launch it. If there are folders in the Applications folder, you'll be able to look inside them too to launch those apps. Most of your apps are now two clicks away!

Using **Grid** view instead of List view isn't a bad option, either. You can use two fingers on your mouse or trackpad to scroll a large grid of icons. It is almost like a pop-up version of Launchpad.

9. Learn About Software Updates

Anything you purchase from the Mac App Store, even items that you get for free, will update through the Mac App Store. You can control how often your Mac checks for updates by going to **System Preferences**, **App Store**. You can also go there to set whether or not app updates are downloaded and installed automatically.

If you'd like to know what has changed in a new version of some piece of software, you can launch the App Store app and go to **Updates**. Then look for the **More** button in the shortened description of the update. Click it to get all the details.

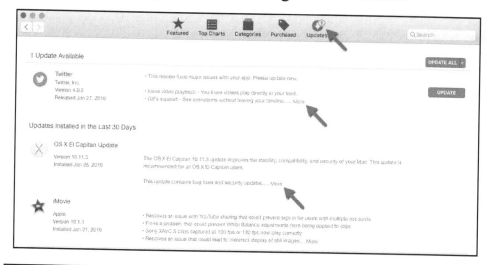

This also works for OS X updates and special security updates, which are included in the list even though OS X isn't technically an "app." Read up on those to get an idea of what has been fixed and what may work differently now.

10. Hide Purchases In the App Store

It is easy to go overboard and download a lot of free apps from the Mac App Store. No harm trying some things out, right?

The problem is that when you go to the App Store App and click **Purchased** you will see everything you have ever downloaded, including little free apps that you may have long ago uninstalled.

You can hide these purchases by going to **Purchased** and then **control+clicking** on an app and selecting **Hide Purchase...**

If you accidentally hid something that you now want to download again, you can go to **Store**, **View My Account**. Log in with your Apple ID. Then look for the **Hidden Items** section which will have a button to **Manage** your hidden items. You'll get a list and can **Unhide** any you wish.

11. Organize Launchpad Apps Into Folders

Even with a modest number of apps, Launchpad can be a bit unwieldy. You can organize it a bit by moving the icons around. Just click and drag the icons to different positions. Drag to the edge of the screen to move from one page to another.

You can also create app folders. This is exactly the same as what most people do with app icons on the Home screen of iPhones and iPads.

To create an app folder, drag one app onto another. You have to drag them pretty much exactly on top of each other or the bottom app will just scoot out of the way of the app you are dragging. You'll see a box outline form behind the bottom app.

Once you drop the app, you'll be prompted to enter a name for the app folder. From that point on, you can drag and drop other apps into it. You can also drag apps out of it.

A little time organizing your apps into folders can save you a lot of time using Launchpad in the long run.

Some apps cannot run independently of others, or they are just apps that you never want to be able to launch from LaunchPad. You can't delete them from Launchpad without uninstalling the app. But you can put them in an app folder to get them out of the way.

12. Speed Up Launchpad Launching

The idea of having a dedicated app launcher in OS X is great for those who want to quickly launch apps. But the experience can be slow if you just click on Launchpad in the Dock, browse the apps, and click the app. If you have a lot of apps, the right one can be hard to find.

Instead of looking, just type the beginning of the app's name. Launchpad's search box at the top will narrow down the results for you. Plus, you don't even need to click in the search box to start. Just typing with Launchpad on the screen will be enough.

So click to launch Launchpad, then type "Calc" and your results will narrow enough to only show the Calculator app. Then press **return** and the app launches.

You can make this a keyboard-only experience by going to **System Preferences, Keyboard, Shortcuts**. Then click **Launchpad & Dock**. Then set a shortcut for **Show Launchpad**. I use **shift+command+space** so it is similar to the Spotlight shortcut of **command+space**. Then I can launch the Reminders app with **shift+command+space, R, E, return**.

If you organize Launchpad into app folders then searching will look both at the main level and within app folders. This means you can put more apps into Launchpad folders and just forget about them. When you need them, search. Meanwhile, your few primary apps can remain on the first screen of Launchpad all lined up and easy to find.

---

13. Delete Apps, Reinstall Later

There are two very useful things that make the Mac App Store different from most previous ways of purchasing software. First, apps that you purchase can be added to all the Macs you own that are capable of running them. The only requirement is that you have to be logged into the Mac App Store using the same Apple ID. In other words, the Mac really needs to be yours.

In the past, this has been an issue for people with a desktop Mac and a MacBook, or maybe a Mac in two locations: home and work, or school dormitory and parents' house. Some software makers have accounted for this, and others just make you buy a second copy or find a creative work-around.

The other useful thing about the Mac App Store is part of the same idea. You can delete an app, and then just install it again later. Once you make a purchase in the Mac App Store, it goes on your Apple account as purchased. If you try to buy it again, you'll just get it for free. You can even go to your Purchased list in the App Store and see **Install** buttons next to these.

This means you don't really have to have a rarely-used app installed at all. You can just install it, use it, and then uninstall it.

You can also do the same with Adobe's Creative Cloud, which features some huge apps that take up a lot of space. I install Adobe Illustrator when I need it, then uninstall it when I'm done.

---

14. The Close Button Knows

Many apps today will auto-save your work. So you can make changes to your current document, quit, and then launch the app again and everything was saved. But if an app doesn't auto-save, it will usually tell you when you have unsaved work in your document with a little hint.

In those apps, look at the red close button at the very upper left corner of your document window. Once you make a change to the document, a dot will appear in the close button. This is your indicator that there are unsaved changes.

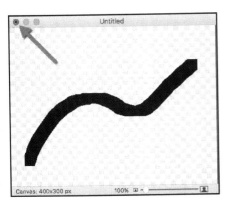

If you click the red close button, it will close the document window. If you hold **option+click**, the app will attempt to close all windows, prompting you if a document needs to be saved first.

15. View Applications By Category

Open up a Finder window and go to your Applications folder. You can do this quickly by using **Go**, **Applications**. Now look in **View**, **Arrange By** and you'll find an item you don't see in other folders: **Application Category**. Choose it and now your apps are sorted by categories. This works in all four Finder views.

Notice that in Icon view, you get all icons in a single row for each category. You can use your mouse or trackpad to flip through the icons horizontally. This also happens with some other **Arrange By** choices, like size. You can also see it when you set regular document folders to arrange by certain criteria using the **View**, **Arrange By** options.

If you are viewing the Applications folder and choose **View**, **Arrange By**, **Date Last Opened**, you will see your apps grouped into Today, Yesterday, Previous 7 Days, Previous 30 Days, and then by years, so you can quickly see your most commonly used apps at the top. You can scroll to the bottom to see which apps you may want to think about uninstalling.

16. Full Screen or Full Screen?

I am often asked about using apps "full screen." This could mean two things in the Mac world. The real full screen function is when everything goes away except the app window. But sometimes you just want the app window to take up all desktop space, but leave the menu bar and other multitasking features in place.

To start, here is a screen shot of a desktop with TextEdit in a window. You can see the menu bar, the Dock, and the desktop background. You can even see another app peeking out from behind.

Now let's choose **View, Enter Full Screen**. The typical keyboard shortcut is **control+command+F**. You can also click the green + button at the top left corner of the window.

'Twas brillig, and the slithy toves
Did gyre and gimble in the wabe;
All mimsy were the borogoves,
And the mome raths outgrabe.

"Beware the Jabberwock, my son!
The jaws that bite, the claws that catch!
Beware the Jubjub bird, and shun
The frumious Bandersnatch!"

He took his vorpal sword in hand:
Long time the manxome foe he sought—
So rested he by the Tumtum tree,
And stood awhile in thought.

And as in uffish thought he stood,
The Jabberwock, with eyes of flame,
Came whiffling through the tulgey wood,
And burbled as it came!

One, two! One, two! And through and through
The vorpal blade went snicker-snack!
He left it dead, and with its head
He went galumphing back.

"And hast thou slain the Jabberwock?
Come to my arms, my beamish boy!
O frabjous day! Callooh! Callay!"
He chortled in his joy.

'Twas brillig, and the slithy toves

Everything is gone except the contents of the window. In this full screen mode, you can bring up the menu bar by simply moving the cursor to the top of the screen. You can even bring up the Dock by going to the bottom of the screen. In addition, if you use Mission Control, then this full screen app now represents a separate Mission Control desktop. You can use **control** plus the **left** or **right** arrow keys to move back to the desktop you were using before, while the full screen app remains in its own space.

To exit this full screen mode, use the same menu command, shortcut, or click the green button that also reappears when you move your cursor to the top.

There is another way to go full screen. Instead of clicking the green + button, hold the **option** key and click the green + button. What this does is expand the window to its maximum reasonable size. The first screen grab shows this. The window fills the top to the bottom, leaving room for the menu bar and

Dock. Some other app that happens to use a wider window would fill all the space from left to right, obscuring everything behind it.

This is a useful mode, too, as it lets you focus on the window without restricting you to just that window. You can still **command+tab** to another app, like the Calculator app shown, and the previous window remains there. Switching back is then even easier.

Instead of **option+clicking** on the green button, you can double-click any empty spot in a window toolbar to do the same thing.

Section 3 — Files and Folders

17. Batch Rename Files

Say you have a bunch of files named Photo A, Photo B and so on. You want to rename them Picture A, Picture B, and so on. You can do this with a batch rename function in the Finder.

As an example, here are three sample files with names like "Doc A.txt." Select them all and then go to **File**, **Rename**. The actual menu item name changes according to the number of files selected.

The Finder window then asks for more information. Choose **Replace Text**, **Add Text**, or **Format**. For this example, select **Replace Text** and then put "Doc" in the **Find** field and "Document" in the **Replace** with field.

Once you click the **Rename** button, all three files will change to use the word "Document" instead of "Doc." If there had been 1,000 files, you could have done this just as easily.

If you choose **Add Text** instead of **Replace Text**, then you get to add text before or after the file name. If you choose **Format,** you get to do things like name all of the files by number or date.

---

18. Compress Files To Save Space and Simplify Searches

Sometimes you have a set of files that are for a specific project. When you are done with that project, you don't need to access those files again in the near future, but you don't necessarily want to delete them, either.

You can easily use the Finder to compress a file, or a folder full of files. Not only may this save some hard drive space, but those files won't show up when you search since they would be hidden away inside a compressed archive.

First, select the file or the folder that you want to compress. Then choose **File, Compress**.

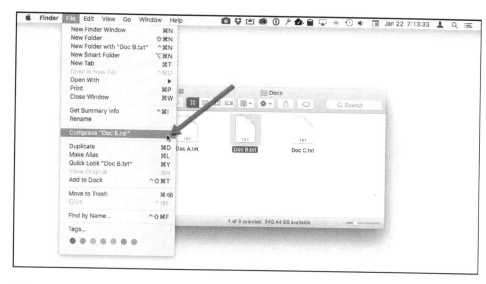

The result is a new file that includes the .zip extension. The original file is still there. You can now put the original in the trash.

This can be used for a single file, like in this example. But it works best when you have a folder full of hundreds or even thousands of files. For instance, as a programmer, I sometimes have groups of large server log files which are just long text documents. When I compress a folder full of them, the resulting .zip file only takes up a fraction of the space.

To uncompress the file, should you ever need to get into it, just **double-click** the file as if you wanted to open it in an app. The Finder will uncompress the archive and give you back your folder or file.

19. The Finder's Inspector

You may know how to "get info" on a file or folder in the Finder. You select the file or folder, then choose **File, Get Info** or press **command+I**. Then you get a little window with all sorts of file information, such as file size.

But what if you want to look at many different files? You could select one, **Get Info**, and then select another, **Get Info**. You could also select them all and **Get Info** and you'll get a bunch of Info windows to sort out.

A good alternative is the Inspector. It looks just like the Get Info window, but with a smaller title bar. To bring it up, select a file and then go to **File, Get Info,** but hold down the **option** key and it changes to **Show Inspector**. You could also just use **option+command+I**.

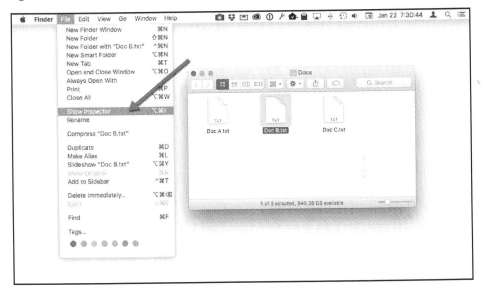

The difference between the Inspector and the Get Info window is that the Inspector shows you the information for any selected file. So select another file and the information in the Inspector changes to show you the information for that second file.

So now you can click and select all around and look over to the Inspector to see what you have.

You can have both the Inspector and regular Get Info windows open at the same time. So if you want to compare files, use a standard Get Info window to keep the information for one file always present, then use an Inspector window to show the information for whatever else you select.

20. Access Your Library Folder

A typical Mac user on a typical day shouldn't need to access the Library folder. But sometimes you need to get into it in order to troubleshoot an app issue or customize something. At some point, you may be following instructions and it will say "go into your user Library folder..."

The problem is that your Library folder is hidden. If you go to your Home folder, you will see Documents, Music, Pictures, Downloads and possibly much more, but no Library. It is there, but Apple is hiding it from you because it can be very easy to get in there and mess things up.

To get to the Library folder, just use the Finder's **Go** menu. Click on that and you'll see a list of common hard drive locations such as Documents, Home, Downloads, Applications, and so on. If you hold down the **option** key while viewing it, then Library appears there, too.

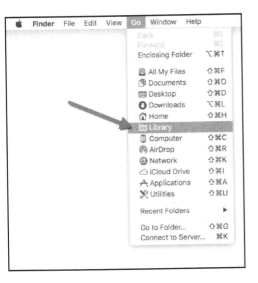

So accessing the user Library folder is as simple as holding the **option** key and then choosing **Go, Library**.

Another way to show the Library folder so it stays visible is to go to the /Users level of your hard drive. Then use **command+J** to bring up the View Options control. You should see an option **Show Library Folder** that you can check.

And remember, there is a reason the Library folder is hidden. It is better left alone unless you have a good specific reason to go into it, and you are following instructions from a source you trust.

Note that this is actually one of two Library folders. The other one is at the top level of your hard drive. This is definitely one to stay away from. But if you need to get to it, you can use **Go, Computer**. Then go into your hard drive's top level from there.

21. Save As... Is Still There

A few versions ago in OS X, Apple changed the File menu for most apps to include things like Duplicate, Rename, Move To, and Revert. This made it easier to perform a variety of file functions without ever leaving the app to go to the Finder. But a lot of users were upset that the Save As... function was missing.

You don't really need the Save As... function, however. You can just use **Duplicate**, which opens up a new document window with a duplicate document. Name it and save it. That's pretty much the same thing. If you then close the original document, then it is exactly the same thing.

However, if you really want it to work like the old Save As... function, you can still do so. Just hold down the **option** key when choosing the **File** menu. The **Duplicate** function changes to **Save As...**

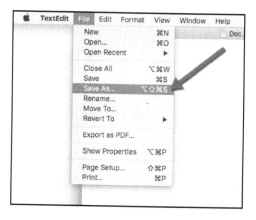

This does make it quicker. And it also has the added benefit of not saving your recent work to the original document. For instance, if you were working in TextEdit and you typed a new line, then without saving the document you used **Save As...** the new line would be in the new file, but not the old one. With **Duplicate**, the new line would remain in the old file as well.

Third-party apps are inconsistent when it comes to Save As functions and Export or Share functions. Some apps will put some file types under Save As and others under Export, and then competing apps will put different ones in each. Graphics editors are particularly bad at this.

22. Delete Immediately

Suppose you want to skip the Trash and delete a file right away. For instance, maybe you just put several items in the Trash and now want to delete something else, but without emptying the entire trash, or maybe you just want to delete a file in one step.

You can do this by selecting the file, folder or group of items, then choosing **File**, **Move To Trash**. But before you release, hold down the **option** key. The menu item will change to **Delete Immediately...**

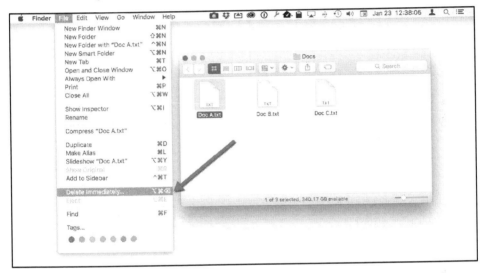

The keyboard shortcut for this is **option+command+delete**.

If you find that you regularly put items in the Trash and then don't want to empty the Trash without reviewing them first, then you probably should review how you delete files. Only put items in the Trash if you are 100 percent sure you want to delete them. Don't use the Trash as a temporary holding place while you decide. If you need that, create another folder in your Documents folder or the Desktop for those files.

23. View File and Folder Sizes

You can see the sizes of all files and folders in a Finder window. The best way to do this is to switch to List view by clicking on the **List View** icon in the Finder toolbar. Then you should see a column for **Size**.

If you don't see the size column, stretch the window to the right to make sure it isn't over there. Also, go to the Finder's View Options controls by selecting **View, Show View Options**. The keyboard shortcut is **command+J**. Then check to make sure the **Size** column is turned on.

One thing that will be missing initially is the size of any folders. There is an option for that as well, called **Calculate all sizes** in the View Options controls.

Once you have this list, you can sort it. Just click on the column head, **Size**, and it will sort in one direction. Click again to reverse the sort.

This can be handy for figuring out which files in a location are using the most space. It can also help you spot things like empty zero-bytes files to get rid of them.

If you are viewing the contents of a folder in a Finder window, you can quickly see how much space the entire contents of the folder uses up by clicking on the folder's background so no files are selected. Then use **File, Get Info** or **command+I** to bring up the Info window and get a file size total.

24. Larger Desktop Icons and Other Options

Remember that the Desktop is just another folder on your hard drive. You can find its actual location in your user home folder. But it has some special properties because the contents of the Desktop folder are mirrored on your actual desktop. Any file you put into your Desktop folder will appear against your desktop background behind all of your windows.

While looking at the Desktop folder in the Finder as a folder, you can view it in list, column, icon, or cover flow view. But the desktop that covers your whole screen is always showing icon view.

You can adjust the size of your Desktop icons by clicking on the desktop to make it the "active window" and then choosing **View, Show View Options**.

Here you can change the icon size, the default grid spacing, and even the text size of the labels. There is also an option to move the text to the right side of the icons.

Choosing **Show item info** will put file sizes under documents and image dimensions under pictures. Unchecking **Show icon preview** will turn all icons to their defaults instead of showing previews of documents as icons.

The **Sort by** option lets you keep the Desktop sorted alphabetically or by some other criteria. An option under Sort by will force the icons to stick to a grid on your desktop instead of staying exactly where you drag them.

25. Show Filename Extensions

By default, OS X does not show filename extensions. These are the (usually) three-character suffix at the end of a filename. For instance, "mybook.doc" has the file extension "doc."

Windows users have been seeing filename extensions since the beginning. But Mac users aren't so used to them. For a while, they were rarely used. Today, they are there, but usually hidden.

To reveal these extensions, go to the Finder. Then choose **Finder**, **Preferences**. Go to **Advanced**. Now check **Show all filename extensions**.

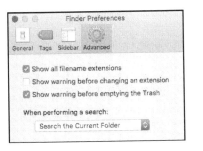

If you had this turned off before, you'll notice the change. For instance, in the Applications folder, "Safari" is now "Safari.app." A Pages document you named "My Book" is now "My Book.pages." Note that OS X doesn't care about the length of an extension, so extensions like "pages" or "numbers" or "keynote" are pretty common.

In addition to this option, you may want to think about the **Show warning before changing an extension** option as well. As a programmer and web developer, I often have a good reason to change the entire filename, including the extension. For instance, I may get a file named "image.JPEG" and want to change it to "image.jpg." The warning can slow me down sometimes.

For most apps, you don't have to worry about adding the extension when creating a file. If you save a file from pages named "My Book Report," it will automatically get the ".pages" added to the end.

26. Duplicate Files With Incrementing Filenames

Say you have a folder with files named "Doc 1," "Doc 2," and "Doc 3." If you select one and use **File**, **Duplicate** or **command+D** to make a copy of it, you will get a file named "Doc 1 copy."

However, if your goal is to create "Doc 4," you can do this in one easy step. Just hold the **option** key down and drag the file, keeping the cursor in the same Finder window, pointed to the same folder. You'll see a green + cursor as you do this. Drop the file and you'll see it is named "Doc 4."

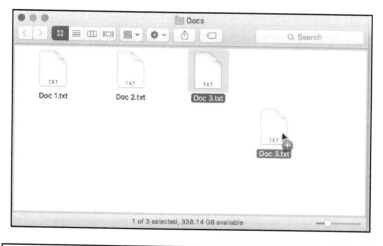

You can do this with multiple files too. So if you were to select all four files after the last step and **option+drag** them, you would get files named "Doc 5" to "Doc 8."

27. Use Emoji Characters In File and Folder Names

I get a lot of questions from people looking to make important folders or files stand out on the Desktop or in crowded folders. Older versions of OS X had labels that would allow you to color the folder and put that color behind the folder or file name, but those have been replaced by tags, which are useful for categorization, but not to get items to stand out.

You could create a custom icon for folders and files, but that takes some work. A quicker way is to simply use a colorful emoji character in the name of the folder or file.

Just edit the file name any way you like, for instance, by selecting the file and pressing the **return** key on your keyboard. Then use **command+control+space** to bring up the special character insertion tool. Then choose a colorful emoji character or anything you like to add some flavor to the name.

If you want to move a single folder or two to the top of an alphabetical list in the Finder, you can do so by adding a space to the beginning of the name, or you could use one of these emoji characters, as OS X will sort them before letters.

28. Copy and Move Files With Keyboard Shortcuts

Mac users know you can drag files to move them. Drag from one Finder window to another. Hold the **option** key down to copy instead of move.

But what if both Finder locations are not visible at the same time?

You can use the same **Copy**, **Cut** and **Paste** commands with the Finder as you do when editing text or images. Select a file or files, then use **command+C** to copy or **command+X** to cut. Then select the new location and use **command+V** to paste. You can even navigate away from the original location before the paste, making it possible to copy or move files while only viewing one location at a time.

You would use Cut to move files and Copy to copy them. One way that this Cut works differently from when manipulating text is that the file or files won't disappear when you first use **command+X**. Instead, the Finder will wait for the **command +V** to remove the files from the original location.

If you move or copy and paste files into a location where there is already a file with the same name, you'll be asked if you wish to replace the existing file or keep both. If you choose the latter, then "copy" will be appended to the filename unless it ends in a number, and then that number will be increased to the next available number.

29. Access File Paths In Finder Windows

It is easy to dig down into folders in the Finder. Just **double-click** the folder and you are inside. But going up can be tougher. Luckily there are ways to do it if you know how.

The simplest is to use **command+↑** to move up one level. But you don't know where you are going until you get there.

However, you can you view the whole path and jump to any level by enabling the path bar. Choose **View**, **Show Path Bar** to enable it. Then you see the path at the bottom and can double-click the folders to jump to them.

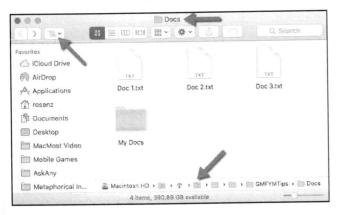

In addition, you can **control+click** the Finder's toolbar and use **Customize Toolbar...** to add a **Path** button. Then you can click for a quick pull-down menu with each part of the path.

Even without these modifications to the Finder window, you can always **control+click** on the folder name at the top of the window to bring up the same pull-down list.

30. Put Back the Trash

If you fill your Trash without emptying it, you could end up with a lot of files in there. You can go into your Trash folder at any time and drag something out of it, but items in the Trash remember where they came from, so you can command them to simply return to the folder they were in originally.

To do this, **control+click** on the item or items in the Trash. Then, from the context menu, select **Put Back**. The item will leave the trash and return, even if you are not viewing that location in the Finder at the moment.

You can also select the file or files and choose **File**, **Put Back**, a special menu command that only works in the Trash folder. The keyboard shortcut is **command+delete**, which is the same command you can use to put items in the Trash. So it is like a double-negative: removing items from being removed.

31. Folder Background Pictures

Everyone knows that you can change your Desktop background. But did you also know you can change the background of any folder in the Finder? Just open the Finder window and go to the folder. You must be in Icon view for this to work, so make sure you are not in List, Column, or Cover Flow view. Then choose **View**, **Show View Options**.

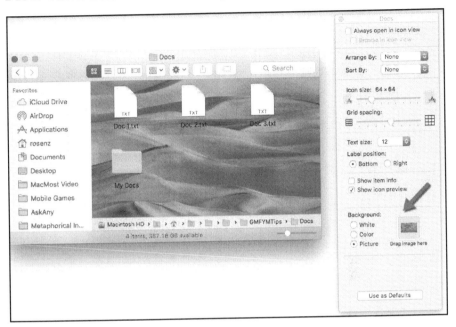

At the bottom of the View Options window, you'll find the Background controls. You can choose a color or a picture. When you select **Picture**, you will see a little square where you can drop any image file. Or, click on the square and you'll be able to select a file starting with the default Desktop backgrounds that come with your Mac.

Sometimes, the change doesn't take place right away, but the background image should appear the next time you view the folder, if not sooner.

In View Options, you can always restore all of the settings to defaults. See that **Use as Defaults** button at the bottom? Hold **option** and it will change to **Restore to Defaults**.

32. Search To Open

When you are inside an app and use **File**, **Open** to open an existing document, you'll find yourself with an open file dialog box that asks you to navigate to the location of the file on your drive to select it. But you don't have to navigate anywhere. You can just use the search box at the upper right if you know the file's name.

You don't even need the file's name, really. The search works the same way it does in the Finder, letting you search for things inside documents as well as the filename.

You can also drag and drop any file or folder into the open file dialog. If you drag a file there, the location will switch to match, and that file will be selected.

33. Resize and Rearrange Columns In List View

The Finder's List View features multiple columns, usually the filename, kind and date last opened. You can resize these

48

columns by clicking and dragging the thin lines between the columns in the header row.

You can also rearrange these columns by clicking and dragging inside the header cells. Move left or right to reorder. If you click without dragging in a column head, it will sort the list by that column. Click again to reverse the sort order.

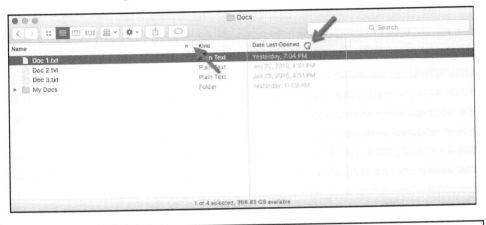

Choose **View, Show View Options** or **command+J** to see a list of all possible columns and add or remove them. You can also change the font and icon sizes here.

34. Column View Previews

The Column View in the Finder is my default. I find it to be the most useful of all of the views. Icon view looks pretty, sometimes. And List View is a good utility for examining the contents of a single folder very closely. But Column View is the best way to navigate through your files and folders.

Another great reason to use Column View is the preview column on the right. It will show you a large preview of the file you have selected, plus lots of information about it. It works for almost any file type, including PDF, for instance. For an image, you can see the dimensions.

To switch to Column View, click its corresponding button in the toolbar or choose **View**, **As Columns**.

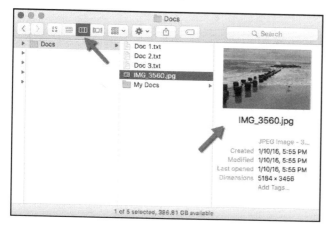

The Preview column will also allow you to watch videos or listen to sounds. If you select a video, you'll see a play button appear if you move the cursor over it.

Having this large preview of images, documents, PDFs, videos and sounds isn't always desirable. It does tend to slow the Finder down a bit, especially as you use the down arrow to flip through items. If you wish to turn off the preview, just choose **View**, **Hide Preview**.

35. Add Apps, Files and Folders To the Finder Toolbar

When you customize the Finder toolbar, you can drag different buttons in and out to make the toolbar more useful to you. Just open a Finder window and choose **View, Customize Toolbar...** But you can also add apps to the Finder toolbar.

To do this, just drag an app from another Finder window to the toolbar while you are in customize mode.

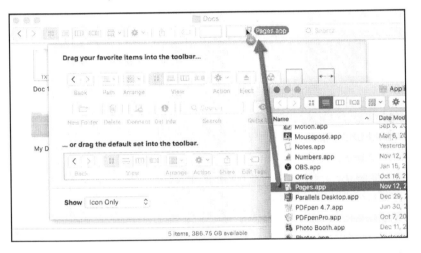

With an app icon in the toolbar, you can now launch that app by clicking on it. You can also open a document by dragging it from the Finder window up to the icon in the toolbar.

You can also do the same thing with files and folders. Drag a file onto the toolbar, and you can now open that file by clicking it. Add a folder, and you can jump to that folder with a click, or drag items into the folder easily.

36. Custom Folder Icons

If you have a lot of folders, you can get lost in a sea of plain blue folder icons. You can actually use any image for a folder's icon, and it is fairly easy to do.

First, select the folder in the Finder. Then choose **File**, **Get Info** or the shortcut **command+I**. At the top of the Info window, you'll see the icon. That's actually a functional area. You can select it and paste an image into it. You can also drag and drop an image file into it.

You can do the same thing with file icons, so if you have a document that you want to stand out, use a custom image instead of the default document icon.

If you are not a graphic artist, you can easily find free folder icons to use. Just do a web search for "free mac folder icons" or something similar and a lot of sites will appear.

37. Finder Tabs

If you work with files, you'll often need to have more than one Finder window open at a time. But there is an alternative. You can have one window open, and then use multiple tabs.

To open a new tab in a Finder window, choose **File**, **New Tab**, or **command+T**. Now you'll see two tabs located at the top of the window. The selected tab's contents are below that. You can click on either tab to switch between them.

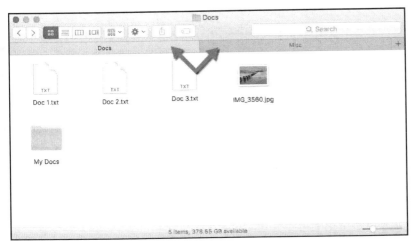

If you need to move a file from one location to another, just drag it from the main portion of the Finder window onto one of the tabs above it, wait a second and the window will switch tabs. Then, drag the file down again to drop it.

You can also drag a tab, moving it out of the current Finder window to make its own window, or you can move them left and right inside the current window to rearrange them. You can have pretty much as many tabs as you want.

If you choose **Window**, **Merge All Windows** in the Finder, then all Finder windows will combine into one, using tabs for each.

38. Deselect Items In a Group

You can select items in the Finder, or almost any app that has objects to select, one at a time with a click. You can select one, then add more by using **command+click** on additional items. You can drag a rectangle to select a group of items.

But did you know you can also deselect items? Say you select a group by dragging a rectangle around them, but there is an item in the middle of this group that you don't wish to include. Now you can **command+click** that item, and it will remove it from the selection. So **command+click** acts as a toggle. It selects items that haven't been selected and deselects items that already have been selected.

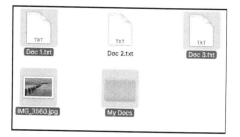

This also works well in conjunction with **command+A** to select all. Say you have a folder with 100 items and you want to delete all but two of them. You can use **command+A** to select all, then **command+click** to deselect the two you want to save. Then drag the selection to the Trash.

You can also drag with the **command** key held down to deselect multiple items from within a selected group.

You can also use the arrow keys in conjunction with the **shift** key to select multiple items in a Finder window. This works best in List or Column View.

39. Always Use the Advanced File Save Dialog

When you go to save a document, you may see a save dialog that looks like this:

This is the basic version of the save dialog. I never use it. By clicking on the little button to the right of the file name, you get the advanced version. It looks like this:

Now you can freely navigate around just like in a Finder window. You even get the sidebar favorites on the left. The pull-down menu labeled Where shows you the current folder and all of its parents. You even have a search field to search for a folder or a sibling file location to get there quickly. And there is a **New Folder** button at the bottom left.

Instead of clicking the little button next to the filename to switch between standard and advanced modes, you can use the keyboard shortcut **command+=**.

If you decide to stick with the standard dialog, you can still do some navigating using the **Where** pull-down menu. It will show your favorites, recent places, and a few other handy locations.

One trick you can perform with the advanced version of the Save dialog is to click on an existing file to steal that file's name, minus the file extension. So if you have a file showing that is "myproject.txt" and you are saving an image from a graphic program, you should be able to click on "myproject.txt," and that inserts "myproject.jpg" into the filename field. Or, if you are saving a text file, you would get "myproject.txt" and then can change that easily to "myproject1.txt" instead of retyping the whole thing.

Section 4 — System Settings

40. Customize Spotlight Search Results

Searches are funny. The more results you get, the less useful they sometimes are. After all, you are most likely after a single file or item. So getting hundreds or thousands of results can make it hard to find that one item.

You can customize Spotlight's results by going to **System Preferences**, **Spotlight**.

If you are like me, you want to use Spotlight to search for applications and files, primarily. So I turn off things like Contacts, Mail, Events and so on. After all, I usually know when I am searching for those specific things, so it is easy to go to those apps and search there rather than use Spotlight.

Going through the options and removing items can make your Spotlight searches so much more manageable. In addition, you can click the **Privacy** tab at the top and then add specific folders that you don't want to appear in search. For instance, if you are a scientist and have a folder with 100,000 text files of lab results, you can add that folder to the privacy list so those files don't clutter up your searches for other documents.

41. Hide the Dock and the Menu Bar

Your Mac's screen is framed at the top by the menu bar and at the bottom by the Dock. The menu bar is necessary since that's how you access primary functions of apps and the Finder. The Dock is mostly necessary, too, as it is the primary way you launch apps, access common items and throw things in the trash.

But both can be hidden and set to only appear when you move the cursor to the top or bottom of the screen.

To hide the Dock, go to **System Preferences**, **Dock** and select **Automatically hide and show the Dock**. You can also use the keyboard shortcut **option+command+D**.

The Dock will disappear. Move the cursor to the very bottom of the screen, and it will spring up for you to use it.

Likewise, you can hide the menu bar. Go to **System Preferences**, **General** and look for **Automatically hide and show the menu bar**. Select and now the menu bar behaves in the same way.

If you look in **System Preferences**, **Keyboard**, **Shortcuts** under the Keyboard category, you'll find shortcuts that let you select menu items from the keyboard. So you can use something like **control+F2**, then arrows, then the spacebar to issue menu commands without using the mouse or trackpad at all. This works even if you have the menu bar hidden, as it will appear as needed.

42. Change Audio Devices From the Menu Bar

If you use your Mac for audio recording, or you just have a set of AirPlay or Bluetooth speakers, you'll need to switch audio inputs and outputs on your Mac from time to time. You can do that right from the menu bar.

Instead of clicking normally on the **speaker icon** in the menu bar, which just allows you to change your volume, you can hold the **option** key down and click it to reveal all of your input and output devices.

This makes it easy to switch without opening System Preferences. You can even jump right to the Sound section of System Preferences with that last item. Note that you must hold down the **option** key before clicking the speaker. The menu won't change if you press the **option** key after clicking.

If you don't see a speaker icon in the menu bar, go to **System Preferences**, **Sound**, and check **Show volume in menu bar**.

If you hold down the **command** key, you can drag menu bar icons like the speaker icon left and right to rearrange them.

43. Adjust Volume In Smaller Increments and With Feedback

Most Mac keyboards have volume adjustment buttons on the top row of keys. You can press these to raise or lower the volume. Depending on your keyboard settings, you may need to hold down the **fn** key on your keyboard for them to work.

But sometimes the jump from one level to the next is too much. To raise or lower the volume in smaller increments, hold **shift +option** down while pressing the volume buttons.

You have even finer control by clicking on the **speaker icon** in the menu bar and then dragging the slider. If you don't see a **speaker icon** in the menu bar, go to **System Preferences, Sound**, and check **Show volume in menu bar**.

The finest control is probably when you go to **System Preferences, Sound, Output**. The slider there is larger, so you can drag it with more control.

If you just hold down the **shift** key when using the volume buttons, you will get some audio feedback as you change the volume. You can also turn on **Play feedback when volume is changed** in **System Preferences, Sound, Sound Effects**.

For advanced users, you can use this command in Terminal to set the output volume to a specific value between 0 and 100:

sudo osascript -e "set Volume output volume 99"

Just replace 99 with any value from 0 to 100. You'll be prompted for your administrator password since this is a sudo command.

---

44. Stop Photos and iTunes From Starting Automatically

When you connect an iPhone or iPad to your Mac, you may find that the Photos app and maybe also iTunes starts automatically. You can turn this off.

First, connect your device and let the apps launch. Then, look for the right checkboxes.

In Photos, click on the name of our device on the left. Then look for the **Open Photos for this device**.

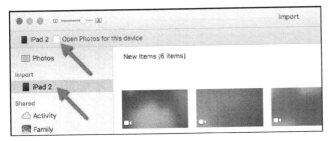

For iTunes, it is a little more involved. Click on the device icon which is usually to the right of the music, video and other icons near the top. Once you have selected your device, click on **Summary**. Then look for the **Open iTunes when this (device) is connected**.

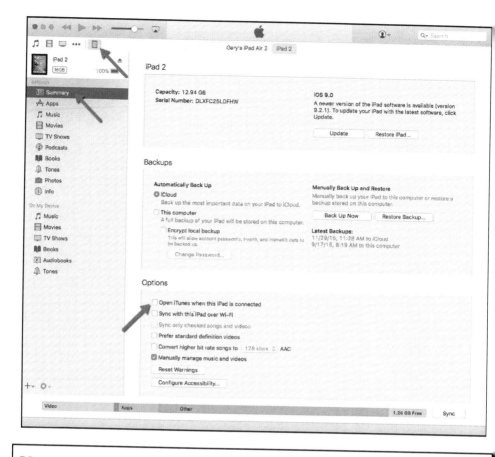

You can actually customize this somewhat to open an alternative app when you connect your device. Launch the Image Capture app that comes with your Mac. It should be in your system's Applications folder. Then look for the device on the left. Select it. Then look for the **Connecting this iPad opens:** menu at the bottom. You can choose any app, such as an alternative photo manager.

45. Show a Message On the Login Screen

Suppose you lose your MacBook and it is found by someone who wants to return it to you. They open it up and are faced with your login screen. They can't get into your Mac, and they shouldn't be able to, but they also have no way to know who it belongs to or how to contact you.

However, you can put a message on that login screen. Go to **System Preferences**, **Security & Privacy**, **General**. Then click the padlock at the bottom right to authenticate yourself as the admin. Next check **Show a message when the screen is locked**. Then, click **Set Lock Message...**

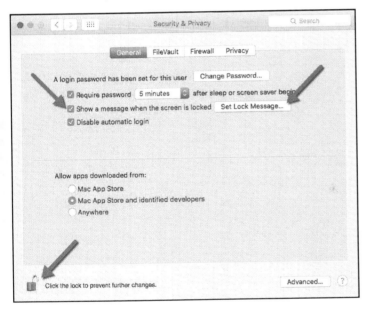

You'll then be prompted to enter a message. You can put your email address or a phone number or anything you want here.

If you have **Find My Mac** turned on in **System Preferences**, **iCloud** (and you should), then you can locate a lost Mac on a map using any computer or device by going to iCloud.com. See http://www.apple.com/icloud/find-my-iphone.html for details.

46. Time Announcements

If you seem to lose track of time while working, you can have your Mac remind you. It can literally tell you the time at regular intervals.

Go to **System Preferences**, **Date & Time**, **Clock**. Then check **Announce the time**. Now you get to choose whether you want to hear these announcements every hour, half-hour or quarter-hour.

Click the **Custom Voice** button to select a speaking voice from your Mac's library. You can even select a speed and volume. So the time can be spoken softly as to not bother people in other offices, or loudly to be heard over your music.

Want to learn to count in a foreign language? You can choose **Customize...** from the bottom of the **Custom Voice** menu and then pick from a variety of non-English languages. Then you'll be asked to confirm if you want to use this language even though your system language is something different. Confirm, and you'll have the time announced in French, Spanish or whichever language you choose. Perhaps choose a slower speed as well. After a few months of hearing the time each hour or 15 minutes in French, you should catch on.

47. Access System Preferences With F-Keys

The top row of your keyboard features special functions like brightness controls and volume controls. You can also use these to quickly access the related System Preferences controls.

First, determine whether you need to use the **fn** key to access these functions. Try the up and down volume keys, usually **F11** and **F12**. If these control the volume with no **fn** key pressed, then you are set. If you need to use the **fn** key for those to control the volume, then note that you'll need the **fn** key for this tip, too. You can toggle between **fn** key settings in **System Preferences, Keyboard, Keyboard**.

Now instead of pressing the volume control keys by themselves, hold down the **option** key. This takes you right to the Sound section of System Preferences.

Likewise, you can access the Display section with the **option** key and either brightness button. You can access Mission

Control preferences with the **option** key and the Mission Control button. If you are using a MacBook with backlit keys, you can use **option** plus the keyboard brightness buttons to get to the Keyboard System Preferences.

The top row of keys seems to change with almost every Mac model. So if your keyboard includes more and different buttons, try them with the **option** key to see if they take you to a place in System Preferences too.

There is no keyboard shortcut to simply launch System Preferences. But you can always access it from the Apple menu, System Preferences. Later in this book, you'll learn how to set up a keyboard shortcut for any menu item.

48. Finding System Preferences

Each section of System Preferences contains many different settings. It can be easy to remember that there is a setting for something, but not know where to look to find it. The search field in System Preferences lets you locate settings by name.

For instance, suppose you remember there is a way to change how the scroll bars work, but you don't know where in System Preferences it is located. Just search for "scrollbar" and it will show you.

Note that the search function is far from perfect. If you search for "hide" to see where you can hide the menu bar, the General settings aren't in the results even though that is where you can find it.

The System Preferences window features backward and forward buttons just like a web browser. The button next to it with a grid of dots is like a browser home button.

49. Customize System Preferences

If your System Preferences are feeling a little crowded, you can always remove items to clean it up a bit. Just choose **View**, **Customize...** Then you'll see checkboxes next to each icon. Uncheck items you want to hide.

Just because they are hidden doesn't mean you can't access them. They will still show up when you use the Search box at the top right. So it may be a good idea to remove the preferences you rarely use to make System Preferences very easy to navigate. Then remember to use Search for anything not listed.

Also, check out **View**, **Organize Alphabetically** for an alternative way to list the icons.

50. Add Handy Notification Center Widgets

The Notification Center appears when you click the menu bar icon at the very upper right corner of your screen, or you can use a gesture as configured in **System Preferences**, **mouse** or **trackpad**. Click the **Today** tab at the top and you'll see the date, calendar events, reminders and some other "widgets" that you can customize.

And boy can you customize! Look at the bottom of the Notification Center and you'll see an **Edit** button. Now you can click any red - buttons to remove widgets. You can add unused widgets on the right with the green + buttons. Chances are you may have some apps that provide widgets you aren't using, like Twitter or iTunes.

In addition, you can click the **App Store** button at the bottom. This takes you right to a special section of the App Store with tons of apps that add widgets. You can track packages, blog, track your bills, tune your guitar and even get a calculator. Look through them all, as you're sure to find something useful.

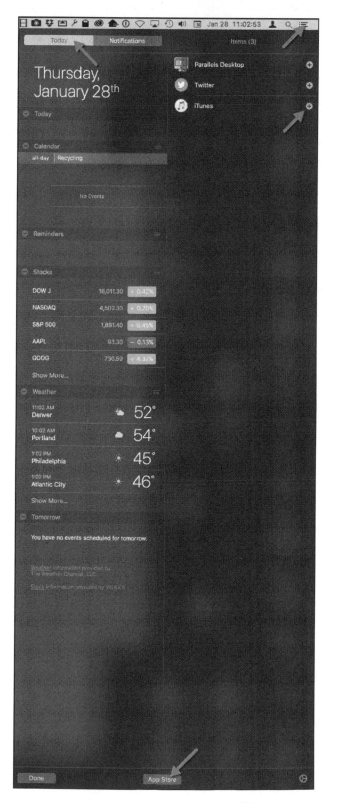

| | Jan 28 11:02:53 |

Today | Notifications

Items (3)

Thursday,
January 28th

Parallels Desktop

Twitter

iTunes

Today

Calendar

all-day | Recycling

No Events

Reminders

Stocks

DOW J | 16,011.30 | + 0.42%
NASDAQ | 4,502.33 | + 0.76%
S&P 500 | 1,891.40 | + 0.45%
AAPL | 93.30 | − 0.13%
GOOG | 730.59 | + 4.37%

Show More...

Weather

11:02 AM
Denver ☁ 52°

10:02 AM
Portland ☁ 54°

1:02 PM
Philadelphia ☀ 45°

1:02 PM
Atlantic City ☀ 46°

Show More...

Tomorrow

You have no events scheduled for tomorrow.

Weather information provided by
The Weather Channel, LLC

Stock information provided by YAHOO!

Done | App Store

While in Edit mode, you can reorder the widgets by dragging the three little lines that appear next to any widget name. This way you can put the important stuff at the top where it will be the most visible.

51. Put Your Mac On a Schedule

Leaving your Mac on while not using it is a good idea because it can take care of system functions, backups, download updates and other things. Just let it go to sleep normally. I never shut down my Mac, but let it sleep.

But if you work in an environment where you are told to shut down your Mac at night, you can at least have it shut itself down and wake itself back up for you.

In **System Preferences**, **Energy Saver,** press the **Schedule...** button. Now you can set a time for it to wake up in the morning and a time to shut down or sleep at night. Just check the boxes and set the times. You can even select **Weekdays** or **Weekends** only.

If you are thinking that this is a good way to force a daughter or son to limit their Mac use, well, it won't quite work that way because it is too easy to override. But you can find controls for that in **System Preferences**, **Parental Controls**. There, you can set time restrictions on a per-user-account basis if you are the administrator. Just make sure the child only has access to their user account and not your administrator one, or they can easily override your settings.

Section 5 — Shortcuts

52. Find Any Menu Item Using Help

The menu bar at the top of your Mac screen changes depending on which app you are using. Some apps have a few very basic menus. Others have many menus, and each menu has many items. Sometimes menu items branch out to include still more menu items!

When menus get numerous and deep, it can be hard to find what you are looking for. But with a little Help, it can be easy. And I mean that literally: Help, as in the Help menu.

Just about every app you use on your Mac includes a Help menu as the last item on the right. Click **Help** and the very first thing you see in the Help menu is a Search field. You may think that the Search field is for searching the help documentation that goes with the app. It does that, but it also will search the names of the menu items to find the one you want.

For instance, say you are using Mail and you want to mark a message as Unread. You remember there is a menu item for that, but don't recall where it is located. So you click **Help**, then type "unread." The result is a list of menu items followed by a list of search topics. In this case, it finds **Sort By > Unread** and **Mark > As Unread**.

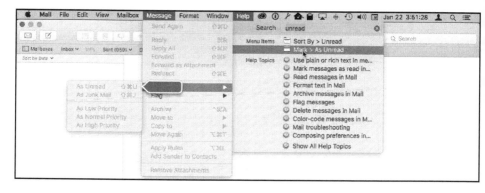

You can move the cursor over the correct menu item and it will show you where that item is located. In this case, it is in **Message**, **Mark**. You can then go to **Message**, **Mark**, **As Unread** to use that function, or you can just select it in the Help menu.

This also helps in situations where you aren't even sure the menu item exists. Just try using the **Help**, **Search** function and typing the names of commands that you suspect may be hidden deep in a menu. Even a partial match will show up. For instance, "unr" will work in this example just as easily as "unread."

You can also access the Help menu search field with a keyboard command. Type **shift+command+/** and it will open the menu and even put the cursor in the search field. So now you can type the name of a menu item and then press **return** to select that item. This gives you keyboard access to any menu item.

53. Switching Between Windows With a Keyboard Shortcut

You probably know that you can switch between apps with **command+tab**. If you are using an app that has multiple windows, you can use **command+`** to switch between those windows. That's the key at the upper left of most keyboards, under the **esc** key.

So suppose you are editing two documents in Pages. You can use **command+`** to switch between them. It also works in the Finder and is a quick way to loop through all of your open Finder windows.

In apps that use tabs, like Safari and the Finder, you can use **control+tab** to move between tabs in the same window.

54. Hot Corners

There are many ways you can create shortcuts for functions on your Mac. For instance, there are keyboard shortcuts and mouse and trackpad gestures. Another way is to use Hot Corners, which are functions triggered when you move your cursor to one of the four corners of your screen.

To set your Hot Corners, go to **System Preferences**, **Mission Control**. Then click the **Hot Corners** button at the bottom left.

You'll then see four pull-down menus, one for each corner. You can use these to select the function that should be performed when the cursor hits that corner.

I like to set the bottom right corner to **Put Display to Sleep**. This makes it easy to shut off my displays as I get up and walk away from my Mac. As I stand up to walk away from my desk, I just swipe my trackpad so the cursor goes down and to the right to activate the Hot Corner.

One Hot Corner command is an anti-command. If you choose **Disable Screen Saver** for a corner, and then put your cursor in that corner, it will prevent the screen saver from launching after a period of inactivity.

55. Create Your Own Keyboard Shortcuts

I am often asked about keyboard shortcuts. People want to know if there is a shortcut for a function within an app. The easiest way to find out is to look at the menu item for that function and see if a shortcut is listed to the right of the item name. If not, that's fine because you can add your own.

To do this, don't look within the app itself. Instead, go to **System Preferences**, **Keyboard**, **Shortcuts**. Then select **App Shortcuts** on the left. Then click the + button.

Now you can choose the application for the shortcut. Usually you want to restrict the keyboard shortcut to a single application. In rare cases, you may want to choose **All Applications**.

Then type the name of the menu item exactly. It must match character for character or your Mac won't know which menu item gets the shortcut.

Then click in the Keyboard Shortcut field and type your shortcut. Make sure you use something that you don't think is in use already. For instance, don't use **command+C** because that's universally used for "copy."

The shortcut should appear instantly in the menu for the app. You can always go back to this System Preferences list and modify your choices, or temporarily disable a shortcut by removing the checkmark next to it. You can also use this to reassign keyboard shortcuts if one already exists for a function.

This works for dynamically-created menu items, too, so you can use it to create keyboard shortcuts for websites in Safari. For instance, if you have "Wikipedia" in your **History** menu, **Bookmarks** menu (including submenus), or as a current window so it shows up in your **Window** menu, then a shortcut assigned to "Wikipedia" will work in Safari. It just has to match the name of some menu item somewhere in the menu.

---

56. Jump To a Document From the Dock

Naturally you can use the Dock to jump to an app or launch it if it isn't already running. But you can also go directly to an open document window by holding down the **control** key before clicking, or using your mouse or trackpad's secondary click.

You actually will see two lists of files. The one at the top is a list of recent documents. These aren't currently open, but you can click one now to open it.

The second list shows the documents currently open, with a checkmark next to the frontmost document for that app. You can click any of these to jump right to that window.

The exact functionality depends on the app. Some third-party apps may not support this as well as Apple's apps. Notice here that TextEdit even has a **New Document** option.

There are two other options in Dock icon context menus that can help you focus on that app. One is **Show All Windows**, which will bring all open windows for that app to the front. The other is the **Hide Others** command, which you can get by holding down the **option** key so **Hide** changes to **Hide Others**. This would hide everything except the windows of that app.

Section 6 — Reading and Writing

57. Quick Access To Your Mac's Dictionary

There are many ways to access definitions from your Mac's dictionary. A very fast method is to select a word and then press **control+option+D**. This brings up a pop-up window with the definition. You'll also get thesaurus entries and other functions. You can just click outside of this window to dismiss it.

You can also get dictionary definitions by using Spotlight. Type **command+space** to open Spotlight, type your word, and then press **command+L** to bypass Spotlight's search functions and jump right to the definition.

You can also, of course, just launch the Dictionary app and look up a word directly in it. While you are there, choose **Go, Front Matter** to reveal all the interesting things that you would normally find in the front or back of a printed dictionary. In the default New Oxford American Dictionary, you get things like a key to pronunciations, spelling and grammar guides, a list of proofreading marks, a list of presidents, a section on the History of English, and all sorts of other reference materials.

58. Easily Type Emoji and Special Characters

I'm often asked about how you type a special character, or add a smiling face to some text. With OS X, this is very easy. Just press **control+command+space** and a little control window pops up with a huge selection of characters.

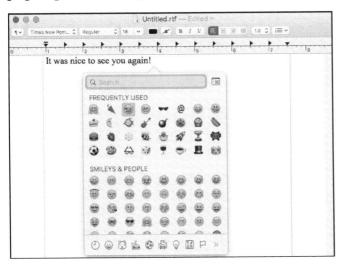

This works in any modern app, such as Mail, Pages, TextEdit (rich text mode only), Messages, and so on. You can click on the categories at the bottom of the window to jump to faces or symbols or flags, and so on.

You can also search. The search box at the top will respond to keywords like "face" or "apple" or "rocket." But sometimes you need to work a little to find the right one. For instance, the standard smiling face comes up if you search for "smiling" but not "smile."

Also note that if you put these in an email and send them to someone using a different operating system, they will see their system's version of the symbol. So your smiling face will look a little different to them, but should still be in the ballpark.

Click on the small button just to the right of the search field to switch to the old character viewer interface that you may recognize from older versions of OS X. The basic functionality is the same, but the old viewer lets you change the size of the emoji to get a better look. You can also drag and drop from the viewer, which can come in handy.

59. Move, Select and Delete Faster

Naturally, you can move back and forward through text with the arrows on your keyboard. One press of the left arrow, for instance, will take you back one character. But you can move faster with modifier keys.

Hold down the **option** key while using the left and right arrows and you will move one word at a time. Hold down the **command** key and you will move to the front or end of the line.

If you use the **option** key with the up and down arrow keys, instead of moving up or down to the next line, you'll move to the start or end of the current paragraph. Press again and you'll be at the start or end of the previous or next paragraph.

If you hold the **shift** key and use the arrows, you will select a character or line at a time. Adding the **option** key makes it a word at a time, and adding the **command** key makes it a paragraph at a time.

The **option** key also works with the **delete** key. Hold it down and you will delete a word at a time. The **command** key lets you delete a line at a time.

You can use the **fn** key with the **delete** key to delete forwards instead of backwards.

60. Quick, Single-Word Translations

You can go to one of many Internet sites to roughly translate text to or from other languages. But sometimes you just want a single word translated. Your Mac's dictionary can do that, and make the function available to you in almost any app.

First, add a translation dictionary in the Dictionary app. Run Dictionary, which you can find in your Applications folder. Then go to **Dictionary**, **Preferences**. Here you can activate more dictionaries that are already available on your Mac. Choose one that is a translation dictionary. You can tell which ones are translation dictionaries by looking for things like (Spanish-English) in the title.

Once added, you can use it in the Dictionary app, of course. But you can also select a word and then use **control+command+D** to bring up the dictionary entry in any app, which will now include the translation.

Another type of translation is to explain technical terms to non-technical people. The Dictionary app can do this as well. Add the "Apple Dictionary" in **Dictionary**, **Preferences** and you can search that for Mac-related terms like "Dock" and "Airport." But don't expect to find other terms like "Bluetooth" or "HDR." Add "Wikipedia" and you'll get definitions for those.

61. Disable the Caps Lock Key

The **Caps Lock** key was useful when people with typewriters needed to put titles on the tops of pages in all caps. But today there is little use for this key unless you want to SHOUT while texting or emailing. In that case, it is more satisfying to slam down and hold that **shift** key while typing anyway, right? RIGHT?

So to disable this waste of space on your keyboard, go to **System Preferences**, **Keyboard**. Then select **Keyboard** at the top. Then press the **Modifier Keys** button.

You'll see all the options for changing what the modifier keys do. Modifier keys are keys that don't type a character on their own, but modify other keys typed.

You can set the Caps Lock key to **No Action,** or you could choose **control**, **option** or **command** to make it a duplicate of one of those keys. Either way, it means you'll never type a password incorrectly because you accidentally turned on Caps Lock.

You may also be tempted to mess around with the other three modifier keys. I don't recommend it. Simply switching the **control** and **command** keys may seem like a good idea for some ex-Windows users, but then one day you'll sit down at another Mac and nothing will seem to work right for you because you'll always be hitting the wrong key.

Instead of disabling the Caps Lock key, would you like to use it as something else? You can, with the help of the app Seil. It is a somewhat technical app not for the casual Mac user. But if you are up for hacking your system a bit, you can use Seil to set the Caps Lock key to do things like launch Mission Control or LaunchPad or mimic one of the F-keys.

https://pqrs.org/osx/karabiner/seil.html.en

62. Text Replacement

This is perhaps the most useful Mac tip you will find anywhere. Do you ever have to type a large piece of text multiple times per day or week? For instance, maybe you commonly respond to an email with a paragraph about needing more information, or maybe you need to type your address or directions on a regular basis. You can set up OS X to take a few characters and replace them with a longer passage.

Go to **System Preferences**, **Keyboard**, **Text**. You'll see a list with **Replace** on the left and **With** on the right. It is already filled with examples, such as replacing (c) with the copyright symbol. You can use the + button at the bottom to add a new entry.

So you could have it replace text such as "reply1" with "Thank you for contacting me. If you would like more information, please fill out the form at my website." Then when you get an email, you can just reply and type "reply1" instead of that entire passage each time.

Some things to keep in mind: First, it sometimes seems to take a minute for new entries and changes to take effect. So if it doesn't work right, give it some time. Second, note that you need to press a space or return after typing for it to work. So if you type "reply1," at first nothing will happen. But hit return and you'll see the replacement.

Also, be sure to make your replacement text unique and something you would never use. For instance, don't use "email" as the trigger text. But "myemail" will work since you wouldn't type those characters without a space after the "y."

If you like this type of functionality, there are many apps that take it even further. Search for TextExpander or TypeIt4Me. Both have a ton of great features that take a few keystrokes and translate them into extended text.

63. Text Transformations

If you ever need to have a block of text transformed from all uppercase to lowercase, or the other way around, you can do it with a simple menu command. Just select the text, then go to **Edit, Transformations**.

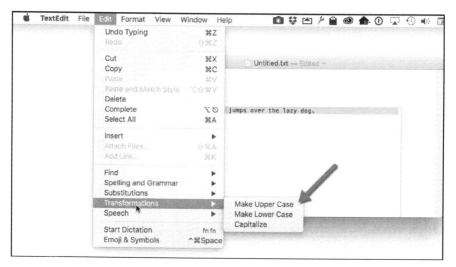

The third option, **Capitalize**, will make the first letter of each word uppercase, and then every other letter lowercase.

Chances are, whichever of these you use, you will need to do some clean-up afterward. For instance, if someone sends you text in all uppercase, you can transform it to all lowercase and then just quickly capitalize the beginning of each sentence, proper nouns, and so on. That's probably faster than retyping the whole thing.

The free text editor TextWrangler in the Mac App Store has a few more options. Using **Text**, **Change Case**, you can capitalize sentences or lines. That's worth getting if you find yourself with pages of all-caps text that you need to get into shape.

---

64. QuickType Words You Don't Know How To Spell

QuickType is kind of like Autocorrect on a mobile phone, but without all the potential embarrassment. Instead of just replacing words as you type, you ask the QuickType function to try to finish a word you have started. For instance, if you type "ency" you can have the rest of the word inserted for you. Just press **esc** or **F5**. Depending on your settings in **System Preferences**, **Keyboard**, you may need to hit **fn+F5**.

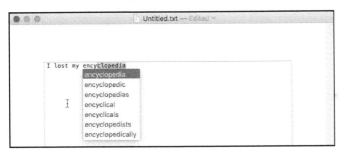

You've got to select the word from the list that appears. But if it is the first word, you can just press **return**. If it is another word, you can use the down arrow to get to it and then press **return**. If there is only one word possible, it skips the list and inserts the word immediately. QuickType can be overridden by some apps, so it won't work everywhere.

In some apps, QuickType will work even without any starting characters. Open a new empty document in TextEdit. Then press **esc**. Then press **space** to accept the first suggestion and then **esc** and **space** again and again. Not very useful, but fun.

65. Have Your Mac Summarize Articles

It seems bizarre that your Mac can do this, but the Summarize function has been around in OS X for a while. It attempts to analyze text and pull out the most important parts based on language analysis.

To enable this function, go to **System Preferences**, **Keyboard**, **Shortcuts**, **Services**. Then look in the list for **Summarize** under the **Text** category. Enable it.

Then go to an article online, or even something you wrote in Pages or TextEdit. Select text and then **control+click**, **Services**, **Summarize**.

This will actually launch a little app called Summary Service. You can use the slider at the bottom to adjust the amount of text in the summary.

Some people use this as a writing tool. After writing a long email or report, you can select it and use **control+click**, **Services**, **Summarize** to see an example of how you might shorten the text.

66. Paste Text Without Styles or Formatting

If you copy a piece of text from a web page or a PDF document, and then paste it into your own document or an email message, the formatting often comes with the text. So you suddenly have a piece of colored, bolded text in a special font in the middle of your otherwise homogeneous text.

You can avoid this by using an alternative to the standard Paste function in the app you are running. For instance, in Mail, you can use **File**, **Paste and Match Style**. The keyboard shortcut is **shift+option+command+V**.

It is the same in Pages, TextEdit and most other Mac apps. However, if you are using a third-party app, you may want to check to see if they call it something else or have a different shortcut.

Section 7 — Using Preview

67. Image Magnifying Glass

You know that part in the detective TV show where they have an image but they just can't make out the license plate number? Then the computer expert hits a key and it enlarges that part of the photo and leads them to the criminal?

Well, you can't really do that. In real life you can't get more detail from an image if it isn't already there. But you can pretend you can with the Magnifier tool in Preview. Just open an image in Preview and choose **Tools, Show Magnifier**. You'll get a circular area that enlarges the part of the image you move your cursor over.

The reason it works here is because the image has far more detail in it than you can see when viewing the entire thing. For instance, a photo taken with an iPhone 6+ is 3264 pixels across. But you may be viewing that in a window that is only 1600 pixels wide. So you can zoom in 2x and see more detail.

This also works with PDFs. But instead of a circle, you get a rectangle. Still, it could make it easier to read the fine-print on those legal contracts.

68. Crop PDFs With Preview

Preview is not just a PDF viewer. You can also manipulate PDFs in many ways, including cropping them to create a new PDF document that contains only the information you need.

As an example, say there is a section of a PDF that you want to email. Open the file in Preview. Click the **Tools** button. Then select the **Selection** button. Now grab the area you want.

Terms: 30 Days

Description	Quantity	Unit Price	Cost
Item 1	55 $	100	$ 5,500
Item 2	13 $	90	$ 1,170
Item 3	25 $	50	$ 1,250
		Subtotal	$ 7,920
	Tax	8.25%	$ 653
		Total	$ 8,573

Thank you for your business. It's a pleasure to work with you on your project.
Your next order will ship in 30 days.

Sincerely yours,

Urna Semper

From here, you can go in one of two directions. You can click that **Crop** button at the top. This will hide the rest of the elements on the page. This is good if you just want to crop and then print.

But if you want to save this as a new PDF, then use **Edit**, **Copy** or **command+C**. Then **File**, **New** from Clipboard or **command +N**. Now you have a new document that neatly contains just what you need. Print, email, save or do whatever you want with it.

I use this all the time for airplane boarding passes. When you print those from the web, you usually get all sorts of ads and other information, sometimes on multiple pages. Instead, I use the **PDF** button on the Print dialog and choose to open it in Preview, so I can go right from Safari to Preview. Then I crop it to just the boarding pass and print that.

69. Merge Two PDFs Into One

Preview lets you merge two or more PDF documents into a single one. To do this, first open both documents in Preview. Then, reveal the left sidebar by clicking on the bottom at the left side of the toolbar. Set it to **Thumbnails**.

Now you should see both documents on the left, separated by a line. If a document is more than one page, look for the little triangle next to it and click it to reveal all the pages.

To merge the two documents, select one or more pages from one, and drag it to the other. Both selection and dragging can be tricky, so if you don't get quite the right result, **Undo** and try again. You can drag individual pages around to reorder them as well. You can merge as many documents as you'd like this way.

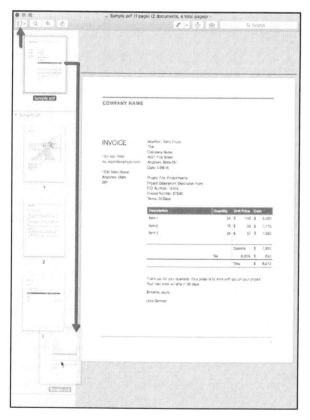

This comes in very handy if you need to combine pages from different types of documents. For instance, you may have a report in Pages and want to combine it with a chart from Numbers and a few slides from Keynote. Just export each as a PDF and then use Preview to merge them.

Note that you can also open Preview documents in separate windows and drag and drop the thumbnails in the sidebars of each window to the other.

You can also just select a single page or set of pages, choose **File**, **New** from Clipboard, and you've got a document with just those pages.

70. Cut Out People and Objects In Photos With Preview

Sure, you can crop photos in Preview, but you can do that in the Photos app as well, which is more likely where you need it. But you can get a little more creative with Preview using the Smart Lasso tool.

Open an image in Preview. Then click the **Tools** button. Then click the **Selection** button and choose **Smart Lasso**. Then click and drag an outline around a person or object in your photo. You don't need to be perfect, but try to get the broad red line to generally fit the outline of the subject.

When you release you'll get a selection that will hopefully match the object. You may need to try again if it isn't quite what you wanted. Sometimes an image doesn't define the object well enough, so it doesn't always work.

Now you can use **Edit, Copy** and take that image and paste it into another. Or use **File, New from Clipboard** to create a new document with just that selection.

Go ahead and cut yourself out of a portrait photograph and paste yourself into another photo to make it look like you are at the bottom of the ocean or sitting on the moon. You know you want to.

You can also use the little magic wand tool, called **Instant Alpha**, to select an area that is the same basic color. Choose that tool and click and drag a short distance in an area of a photo. A red color will show the area being selected. Release and you've selected that area and can copy and paste from there, or press **delete** to remove that area from the photo. This works best when there are two contrasting areas in the photo, like a yellow flower on a green background.

71. Create a Top-Secret Encrypted PDF

Preview lets you save an open PDF as an encrypted one, with a password and everything. Anyone would then need this password to open the PDF. It isn't just "locked" but actually encrypted, so unless a spy agency wants to devote some time and resources to it, the document is pretty safe from prying eyes.

With the document open, choose **File, Export**. Make sure the format is set as **PDF** and then check **Encrypt**. Now you'll need to enter a password. And then a second time for verification.

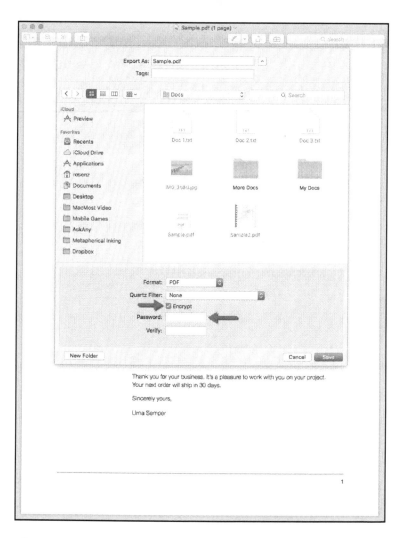

If you save this over your existing PDF, or simply delete the original, keep in mind that the only way to open your encrypted copy is to enter the password. If you forget the password, no one can help.

This can also be used with images. You can open an image with Preview, save it as a PDF and select **Encrypt**. The result will be a PDF with the image embedded inside.

Section 8 — Using Safari

72. Safari Tabs

Even casual Internet users like to have more than one Safari window open at a time. You could be reading news in one, checking Facebook in another and shopping in a third. But expert Safari users will just have these open in a single window, each in its own tab.

To start a new tab in Safari, use **File**, **New Tab** or **command +T**. You can switch between tabs by clicking on them near the top of the Safari window. Each tab acts like an independent window, but grouped together so as not to clutter your desktop with windows.

To select any tab, click it. To remove a tab, move your cursor to it and look for the small **x** button. The tab doesn't have to be the active one for you to use the **x** button.

The key to using tabs efficiently is to be able to create them at will. Go to **Safari**, **Preferences**, **Tabs** and look at the options. Typically, you can **command+click** on a link to open a new tab. You also have the option to turn off "When a new tab or window opens, make it active." Now when you are looking at a list of links or search results, you can **command+click** in the list and open a series of tabs. The pages load in those tabs at the same time. Now you can go through each one and look at those web pages. All this time, your original list or search results are in the first tab, ready for you to access again.

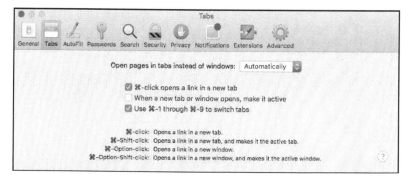

You can use the **command** key and a number to jump to a tab in the current window, so the first tab would be **command+1**, the second tab would be **command+2**, and so on. You can use **control+tab** and **shift+control+tab** to move to the next and previous tabs, respectively.

73. Open a Set of Web Pages In Tabs

This tip combines the idea of Safari browser tabs and bookmark folders. Suppose you have a morning routine that involves reading several news websites. You go to one, then another, then another. Maybe you already have these sites bookmarked.

If you put these bookmarks into one bookmarks folder, you can open them all at once with one command. First, use **Bookmarks**, **Show Bookmarks** to organize them into a single folder. For this example, I'll call a bookmarks folder "Morning News."

Now when you want to read all of your morning news, just go to **Bookmarks**, **Morning News**, **Open in New Tabs**. This will open all the sites, each in its own tab. As you read one, the others will load in the background and be ready and waiting.

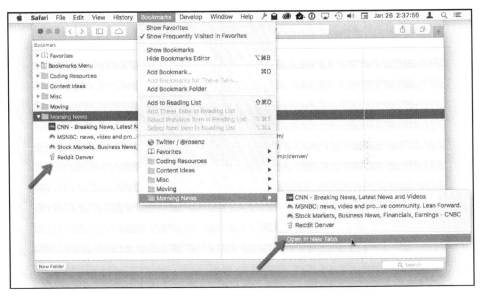

This is also great for complex multi-page work tasks. For instance, say you need to check a group of several reports multiple times per day. Put links to all of those web pages into a folder and use **Open in New Tabs** to access them all at once.

You can also use this with bookmarks in the Favorites bar at the top of Safari. When you select the Favorites bar folder, you'll see **Open in New Tabs** at the bottom of the list that appears making it even easier to access all those pages quickly.

74. Search Results SnapBack

Say you search for something on the web and then click on one of the results. You then continue to click, maybe reading multiple pages on that site, maybe following links to elsewhere. Then you decide you want to go back to your search results and try another page from there.

You could just redo the search. But if your search terms were complex, that is easier said than done. So instead, use Safari's SnapBack feature. Choose **History**, **Search Results SnapBack**.

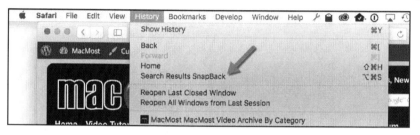

This takes you right back to the results page. Memorizing the keyboard shortcut, **option+command+S** is definitely worthwhile if you are like me and perform dozens, if not hundreds of searches per day.

> Want to remember what you searched for yesterday, last week or last month? If you are signed in to your Google account, and you go to https://history.google.com, you can see your Google search history.

75. Search Your Browser History

Did you want to find a web page you recently visited, but can't remember the URL or site name? No need to search the entire Internet again. Just search your browser history.

Bring up the History window by choosing **History**, **Show History**. Then look for the little search field at the bottom right. Type your term in there and you'll get a list of pages you have recently visited that match.

As long as you are using iCloud and have **Safari** checked in **System Preferences**, **iCloud**, your history will sync between your devices. So you'll even be able to search the history of sites you visited on your MacBook while on your iMac. iOS history will be there, too.

76. View Full URLs In Safari

By default, Safari will only display the domain of the website you are on. So no matter how deep you are in a site, you still just see something like "thesitename.com."

If you are like me, you want to know the whole thing. You could just click on the address field, which will reveal the full name, or you could turn off this less-than-useful feature in **Safari**, **Preferences**, **Advanced**. Look for **Show full website address** and check it.

Likewise, if you go to **View**, **Show Status Bar**, you can turn on a feature that displays the full URL of links as you move the cursor over them. Look for these URLs at the very bottom left corner of the Safari window.

77. Search Inside a Webpage

So you search for some information on the web. You find a page that might have what you are looking for. Problem is, the page is huge. How can you zero in on the part of the page that has what you want?

The way to do that is to search inside that web page. Safari makes it easy. Just choose **Edit**, **Find**, **Find...** or the shortcut **command+F**. Now you get a small search box at the upper right corner of the screen. Type in a search term there and you'll get the number of matches to the left of that, plus some arrow buttons so you can move between those matches.

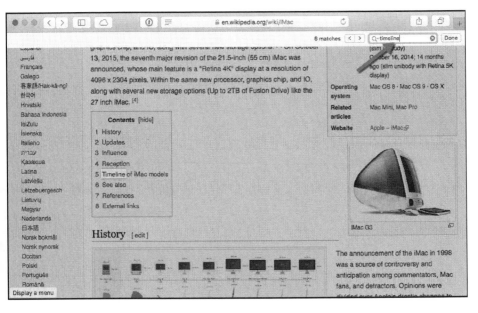

When you find what you want, hit the **Done** button to dismiss the search toolbar.

If you want to flip through the matches quickly, use **command +G** to go to the next match and **shift+comment+G** to go to the previous match.

78. Pause and Resume Downloads

If you are downloading something in Safari, you have the option to pause and resume the download while it is in progress. To do this, bring up the Downloads list by going to **View**, **Show Downloads**, or click on the icon in the toolbar.

Click on the **x** button that appears next to the item when you move your cursor over it. Once you do, the download stops. But the **x** button is replaced with a **resume** button. You don't have to stay on the web page to resume the download. As long as the file isn't removed from the server, you can resume at any time by using that **resume** button.

If you'd rather remove the item from the list completely, you can do so by **control+clicking** on it and choosing **Remove From List.**

79. Mess Around With Safari's Develop Menu

Go to **Safari, Preferences, Advanced** and check the last item called **Show Develop menu in menu bar**. This gives you a new menu at the top of the screen. In it, you'll find all sorts of goodies.

You can empty the cache, which used to be a regular menu command on earlier versions of Safari. You can also disable the cache if you are having difficulty with a website.

You can easily disable images if you need to access the web on a very slow connection, like on the free wifi at an airport.

You can also bring up Safari's detailed programming tools using the **Develop** menu. Even if you are not a programmer, this could be useful. For instance, if you bring up the **Error Console,** you can get information that can help you report a website bug to the site's owner.

80. Follow News In Safari With RSS Feeds

Syndicated news feeds were a popular way to see the new articles at a website for many years. Then Apple removed RSS functionality from Safari and Mail for a while. But in El Capitan, RSS has made a return.

To add an RSS feed to your sidebar in Safari, first go to a website that has RSS feeds and makes them properly available in the site headers. Many news sites do this, but some do not.

Then open the sidebar by clicking the **Show Sidebar** button. Click the @ button to go to the Shared Links section of the sidebar. At the bottom of the sidebar, you should see a **Subscriptions** button. Click that, then click **Add Feed**.

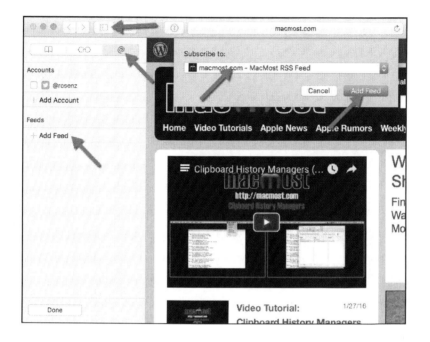

You'll be shown a control with a pull-down menu that lists RSS feeds found. Many sites have more than one, so select the one you want. Then click **Add Feed**. Finally, click the **Done** button at the bottom left.

Now when you view the Shared Links section of the Safari sidebar, you'll see all the recent items in all the RSS feeds you have added. That's a handy way to check the news from sources you care about.

You can also use the **Add Account** button to add your own Twitter account to the Shared Links sidebar. Then you'll see all incoming tweets alongside the RSS items. For sites that don't have RSS feeds, but have Twitter accounts, you can always create a second Twitter account and only subscribe to those news sources. Then add that Twitter account to your sidebar to see those items.

81. Quick Access To Sites With Pinned Tabs

Safari in El Capitan introduced a new way to quickly access pages you use often. When you are viewing such a page, choose **Window**, **Pin Tab**. Now you'll see a small tab on the left side that represents the current tab you are viewing, even if it is the only tab you have open at the moment.

The best part of pinned tabs, as opposed to regular tabs, is that they are persistent. They are always there. So every Safari window you open will show the pinned tab to the left, and you can easily access it.

In addition, pinned tabs stay in sync across browser windows. So if you navigate to another page in one window and then switch to the other window and go to the same pinned tab there, you'll see the same page. And this page will be remembered even if you close the window.

So, for instance, say you use a pinned tab to access your local newspaper site. Then you click on a link to read an article. Then you close that window. Next time you go to that pinned tab, it will start at that article. This is very different from bookmarks or other ways of remembering pages, which will always take you back to the initial page when you use it.

82. Control Web Page Plugin Content

There is a lot of good web content out there requiring you to have a plugin installed in Safari to view. Flash is the most common. But unfortunately, Flash is also used by the most annoying and resource-intensive web ads.

With the help of a Safari extension, you can make Flash content load only when you give it permission. This gives you all the good Flash stuff you want, like games, and you can avoid it when you don't want to see it.

To do this, add the Safari extension ClickToPlugin. You can get it at https://hoyois.github.io/safariextensions/clicktoplugin/

Just download the latest version and double-click it to add to your Safari extensions. Once you do, you'll need to click on plugin content for it to load.

It also gives you a ton of settings which you can access by going to **Safari, Preferences, Extensions** and then clicking on the option to launch the ClickToPlugin settings.

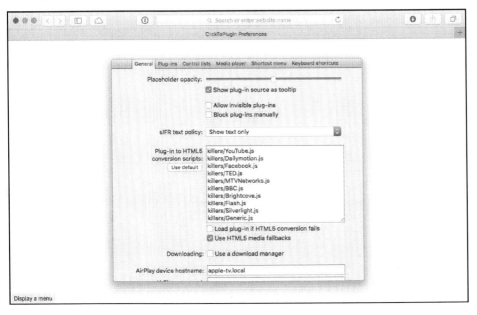

If you really want to control the specifics now, you can. You can set your favorite Flash game sites to load Flash automatically, while other sites show the option to click. You can add keyboard shortcuts and all sorts of options.

ClickToPlugin also allows you to define a default video player. Many websites will provide both Flash and simple HTML5 video. If you go to the ClickToPlugin extension settings under Media player, you can define the default as HTML5 or Plugin (Flash, usually). Note, however, that most features of advanced video players, like YouTube videos, will only be available in the Flash player.

83. Use Reader View To Focus On an Article

Safari's Reader View gets rid of all of the ads, navigation bars and other content and allows you to focus on the article or other content on a page. It is only available if Safari can figure out which part of the page is an "article" so you won't always see it. But when it is available, you'll see a special icon at the top of the Safari window, in the left side of the address field.

Once you are in Reader View, you can click on the right side of the address field where a small AA button appears. Use this to set the font size, font face and the background color.

To exit Reader View, click the first button again, or it goes away by itself if you leave the page.

While in Reader View, you can use **command+=** and **command+-** to increase or decrease the size of the text. Use **command+0** to return to the default size.

84. Search Within a Single Site

This tip isn't specific to the Mac, but will work anywhere you browse the web. It is so useful, though, that I will include it anyway.

If you want to search for something on the web, and know which website you will likely find it on, you can tell Google to search only that website.

The simple trick is to use "site:" and the site's domain name before the search. For instance "site:cnn.com election poll results."

You can even go deeper than the site. For instance, to search the forum at MacMost.com, you can use "site:macmost.com/forum safari bookmarks."

85. Private Browsing For Unbiased Results

When you hear the term "private browsing," you may think about web sites not tracking you, cookies not being saved, ads not being customized to you, and so on. But the main reason I use private browsing mode in Safari is to get unbiased search results.

If you are using Google as your search engine and are logged into Gmail or any Google service, you will get search results tailored to you. Most of the time that means better search results. But sometimes I want to see what other people are seeing.

To switch to private browsing mode in Safari, choose **File**, **New Private Window**. Then use that window to search. Compare the exact same search with a non-private window. You can do it side-by-side.

Plus, pages you visit while using private browsing are not saved in your history. So if you use your history to help with research at school or work, and then want to take a break and read some news, those pages you visit won't add to your web history.

86. Drag and Drop to Upload Files

Say you are on a web page that is prompting you to upload a file. You see the usual **Choose Files** button. You can click it, and then browse to find the file, select it, and then press Choose to upload.

But now you'll never do that again because I'm going to tell you an easier way. You can drag and drop a file from a Finder window to the **Choose Files** button.

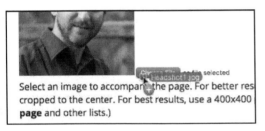

Select an image to accompan the page. For better res
cropped to the center. For best results, use a 400x400
page and other lists.)

When you do this, you'll see a green + cursor appear as you properly position the cursor with the file over the **Choose Files** button. Drop it there and it saves you all the trouble.

If you click the **Choose Files** button, you get a normal-looking file open dialog. This includes a **Media** category in the left sidebar. Under that, look for the **Photos** item. Click it and you can browse your Photos library for an image to upload directly from your library to the website without needing to export it to a file first.

87. Resize Text Areas

Sometimes when you fill out a form in Safari, you are faced with a small text field. Not the one-line kind, but the multi-line text fields known to developers by the HTML tag <textarea>.

They are very common, and usually where you spend a lot of time because you are being asked to enter in a considerable amount of text.

You can expand these text fields in Safari when you see the diagonal lines in the very bottom right corner. Just click there and drag the field down and/or to the right. Usually, you can't make the field any smaller than the original size, but you can almost always make it larger.

http://macmost.com/e-1169 Perhaps one of the most useful things you can add to your app is a clipboard history manager. Take a look at two free apps that allow you to recall multiple clipboard items, not just the current text in the clipboard buffer. Any Mac user should find Jumpcut or ClipMenu useful additions to their computer.

Whenever I am asked to type a lot of text into one of these text areas, I always switch to TextEdit or Pages and write the text there. It is much easier to write in a real word processor, and it is easy to copy and paste the text when I am done. I don't get rid of the document right away, either, in case there is a problem with the web form when I try to submit.

88. One Small Setting Change To Improve Security

While Safari is generally a safe browser, and the default options are good ones, there is one option I recommend changing. If you go into **Safari**, **Preferences**, **General**, you'll see it at the bottom. Uncheck **Open "safe" files after downloading**.

What this does is automatically open files like videos or PDFs when you download them. So you click on a link that says "download this PDF," and the next thing you know, Preview launches and there is the PDF. Very convenient. And dangerous.

In the past, some of the more advanced file types like videos and PDFs have been used to do malicious things. And some websites have been hijacked to trick you into downloading these. All that unchecking this does is add an extra step for you when you download a legitimate file. You'll then need to look in your Downloads folder and double-click it to open it.

But if you download a file you did not want, that you were tricked into downloading by a bad link or website code, it will just sit harmlessly in your Downloads folder until you delete it.

I know of no malware threats at the moment that use this technique. But it has happened in the past. So why not turn off this small setting and give yourself a little barrier between your computer and an unwanted download?

You can also change **File download location** to **Ask for each download** if you want even more protection. This gives you the chance to use the **Cancel** button before anything is downloaded. But it can be annoying to have to specify a location every time you want to download a file.

89. Control Safari Website Notifications

Sick of going to websites only to find everything frozen because an alert has appeared asking if you want to receive notifications from that website? You can silence those alerts by going to **Safari**, **Preferences**, **Notifications** and unchecking **Allow websites to ask for permission to send push notifications**.

The controls here also allow you to **Allow** or **Deny** notifications from any site that has requested it. So no matter which way you answered the alert originally, you can switch it here.

You can select any item and use the **Remove** button to get it out of the list entirely. But if you leave the checkbox checked, and remove the item from the list, you'll just get an alert again the next time you visit that site since it is acting like you have never been asked before.

---

90. Mute Tabs In Safari

If you use multiple tabs in Safari, you may occasionally run into a situation where you hear sound start playing, but you don't see any video or audio player on the web page you are viewing.

The sound is most likely coming from another tab. Sometimes, it is an obvious tab with a video as the page content. Sometimes, it is an annoying advertisement that didn't start while you were viewing the page, but has now started while you are on another tab.

Safari gives you a clue as to which tabs are playing sound. Look at the right side of the tab and you'll see a little speaker icon.

You can switch to the tab and stop the media from playing, or you can click the speaker icon to mute the sound in the tab. You can also **control+click** to bring up a list of all of the tabs that have sound playing.

If you have multiple tabs with sound playing, you can click on the speaker icon on the current tab and you'll see an additional option to **Mute other tabs**. Then you'll only get the sound from the tab you want.

---

91. Private Browsing For Multiple Logins

Some people think, incorrectly, that when you are in private browsing mode, no cookies are saved. Not true. They are saved, but they are separate from your regular cookies. Plus, they are destroyed when you close the private browser window.

The upshot of this is that the private window acts like a completely different browser instance. So if you have, say, two Gmail accounts, you can remain logged into your main one in Safari while you open a private browsing window and log into the other account. Both windows behave like two separate browser apps in this case.

Likewise, you can use two or more accounts from any site this way. Or, no account at all. For instance, you can remain logged in to your YouTube or Facebook account and also see what a non-logged-in user will see when they visit your YouTube or Facebook page.

To open a private browsing window in Safari, choose **File**, **New Private Window**.

If you ever find that a website doesn't work right in Safari, you can always try it in another browser. The second and third most popular browsers for the Mac are Chrome and Firefox. Both are free and easy to install. Web developers usually have all three browsers installed on their Macs.

Section 9 — Miscellany

92. Use a Solid Color As a Desktop Background

Most of the Mac desktops I see use the default desktop background that Apple supplies. It is beautiful, but I prefer to concentrate on my work. So instead of switching to another Apple image, or even using one of my own photos, I opt to use a solid black background.

To do this, go to **System Preferences**, **Desktop & Screen Saver**. Then choose **Solid Colors** on the left. You'll see a set of colors, none of which are solid black. So click the **Custom Color** button.

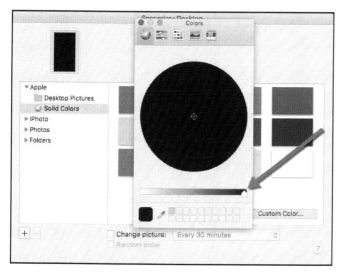

When you click this button you get the Apple Color Picker, a dialog that you see throughout Apple apps that allows you to pick colors in different ways. Using the first option, the color wheel, I simply drag the bottom slider to the right to get to solid black.

Solid black isn't for everyone. You may want to experiment with the default colors that Apple gives you.

You can also just try a different picture. That little box at the top of the System Preferences window with the picture in it can be used to drag and drop any image to make it your desktop background. So, for instance, you can download space pictures from NASA (https://www.nasa.gov/multimedia/imagegallery/index.html) and make them your desktop background.

93. Use Spotlight As a Calculator

You can click the magnifying glass at the top right corner of your screen to access spotlight and search for files. A quicker way is to use **command+space**.

Spotlight can be used for much more than searches. You can use it as a calculator. Just type in the math equation you want. Try 2+2.

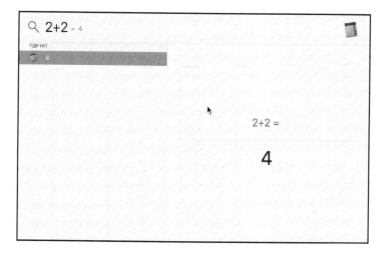

Spotlight's calculator function has some advantages over the Mac's Calculator app. You can use parenthesis to perform more complex calculations. You can then edit those equations to try variations.

You can also use common mathematical functions like sin, cos, log, sqrt and so on.

```
Q  sqrt(625) = 25
TOP HIT
   25

           sqrt(625) =
              25
```

A regular calculator, even the Calculator app on your Mac, has a memory function. So does spotlight. Just use **command+C**. You don't need to select the text first. Then **command+V** will paste as you would expect. Of course, you can also paste the answer outside of Spotlight this way, too.

94. Scientific and Programmer Calculators

You probably are familiar with your Mac's calculator app. Just look in your Applications folder or search for it. You get a basic calculator. But it also has two advanced modes.

The first is the scientific calculator. Go to **View**, **Scientific** to switch to it. Here you get some more advanced functions like the calculators used by college students.

You can also switch to RPN, or reverse polish notation, by choosing **View**, **RPN Mode**. If you don't know what that is, then you probably don't need to bother with it.

Another calculator is the programmer one. Choose **View**, **Programmer**. Now you get functions that are commonly used by coders and other computer users.

This can even be used by graphic artists. If you look at the three buttons labeled **8, 10, 16**, these let you convert between octal, decimal and hexadecimal. Sometimes colors are described with decimal or hexadecimal numbers and you can convert between them by clicking those buttons. So an RGB value of 240,216,64 can be converted by entering 240 in decimal (**10**) mode. Then clicking **16** to switch to hexadecimal to show 0xF0. The number 216 gives you 0xD8 and 64 gives you 0x40. So 240,216,64 is the color #F0D840.

Note that you don't need to use the mouse or trackpad to enter numbers with the Calculator app. You can use the keyboard. You can use the +, - and = keys, too, as well as / for division and * for multiplication.

95. Watch Videos at a Faster Pace

If you are viewing a video in the QuickTime Player app, you can click the >> button to fast forward. Click it again and the speed gets faster. This is useful for getting to another point in the video, but what if you wanted to simply speed things up a bit to digest the video at a quicker pace?

You can increment the speed at a smaller amount by holding the **option** key and clicking the >> button.

Now you'll get speeds like 1.1x and 1.2x, all the way up to 1.9x. At these speeds, the audio stays on and speeds up along with the video. Plus, QuickTime Player will keep the pitch of the audio steady, so the voices don't sound like chipmunks.

At 2x, the audio will cut out and the playback will act like normal 2x speed.

Did you know you can drag the playback controls in QuickTime Player to any position in the window? Just click in a spot that doesn't have a button and drag. You can get it out of the way in case there are subtitles or other text under that spot.

96. Two Ways To Convert Currencies

You can get a quick currency conversion on your Mac using either Spotlight or the Calculator app.

With Spotlight, just type things like "5 euros" or "5 gbp" or "5 swiss francs." You'll get a Spotlight menu that uses up-to-the-minute rates. Combine this with the **command+space** shortcut to access the Spotlight menu, and you can get conversions in a second.

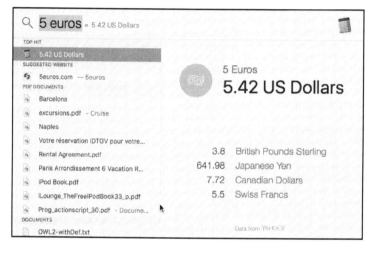

You can also do this with the Calculator app. Just type the number and choose **Convert**, **Currency...** then select the **From** and **To** options.

Note that you can convert a lot more than just currencies in both Spotlight and Calculator. Try typing things like "5 meters" or "76 lbs" in Spotlight. And look at the list of items in the Calculator's **Convert** menu.

97. Swap Left and Right Speakers

If you have an unusual audio setup with external speakers, and you find that the left and right speakers are on the wrong sides, you can tell your Mac to swap them without needing to rewire anything. Look for the app Audio MIDI Setup in the Applications/Utilities folder and launch it.

Then click on your output on the left and click **Configure Speakers...** at the bottom.

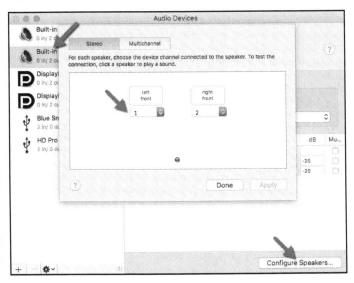

Now you can set the left speaker to carry channel 2 instead of 1, and the right speaker to carry channel 1 instead of 2. Then click **Done**.

You can also set the volume for each channel. So if one speaker is obscured and the other is not, you can manually adjust them to get a better mix from where you sit.

98. Windows Resizing Tricks

To resize a window, you can click and drag the edges or the corners. You can resize in special ways by dragging the corners while holding down modifier keys.

Drag one side while holding the **option** key, and both that side and the opposite side will move. Drag one side while holding down the **shift** key and the current side, plus the two adjacent sides will move. Hold both the **option** and **shift** keys, and all four sides will move, keeping the window centered at its current location.

Hold **shift** and drag a corner, and the window will resize but keep its current width/height ratio. Hold **option** and drag a corner, and both that corner and the opposite corner will move. Hold both **option** and **shift** while dragging a corner, and the window will keep both its center and ratio.

One great thing about holding **option** and dragging a side is that the edges of the window will lock to the edge of the current screen. So if you have a multi-screen desktop setup, you can use this to make a window exactly fill the width or height of a screen without overflowing into the next screen.

99. Click With Pixel-Perfect Precision

You may already know about OS X's Accessibility Zoom function. This allows you to zoom in to enlarge part of your screen. Turn it on by going to **System Preferences**, **Accessibility**, **Zoom**. There are tons of options. If you have never used it before, turn on the keyboard shortcuts and try them. Also try the gesture controls.

While some people love to use this feature, for others, using the entire screen is too much. So instead, you can use the Zoom Style **Picture-in-Picture** to create a rectangular magnifying glass when you need to select with pixel-perfect precision in graphics apps.

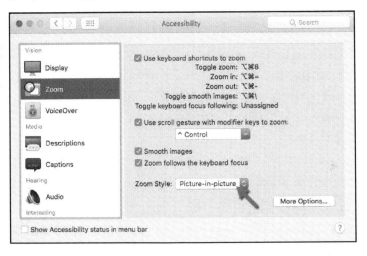

Now you can bring up this magnifying glass for a few seconds, and easily dismiss it. In fact, if you click on **More Options...,** you can select an option to **Enable temporary zoom** by holding down the **control+option** keys. However, this also means you have **control+option** held down when you click. I find that with a trackpad, I can position the cursor, release **control+option,** and then click to get the pixel I want.

Inside **More Options…,** you can click on **Adjust Size and Location** to make the magnifying glass larger or smaller. You can also set a location and use the **Window Position: Stationary** option to always keep the magnified view in the same place on your screen.

Whether you use a stationary window or one that moves with the cursor, you can adjust the width and height of the rectangle using **shift+control+option+arrows**. You can also simply use **control+option+arrows** to nudge the window in any direction.

100. Talk To Your Mac

The keyboard and mouse aren't the only ways to enter input into your Mac. You can also use the microphone. To enable dictation, go to **System Preferences, Dictation & Speech, Dictation**. Turn on dictation and select a language and shortcut.

To test it out, create an empty TextEdit document. Use the shortcut, and speak.

If you enabled **Use Enhanced Dictation**, you can edit with the keyboard as you speak. Once you get used to this hybrid fashion of typing, you can enter text pretty quickly. Works in pretty much any app. So you can use it to compose emails, fill out forms online, or write your next novel in Pages.

101. Let Your Mac Talk To You

Text to speech functionality has been around on Macs for years, even predating OS X. But a lot of people still don't use it. It is possible to have your Mac easily read news articles to you from the web, or speak your incoming email.

Enable this by going to **System Preferences**, **Dictation & Speech**, **Text to Speech**. Check the box **Speak selected text when the key is pressed**. You can also select a voice and speaking rate, and test it out with the Play button.

Now try selecting some text in your web browser and using the shortcut key specified in System Preferences to have the text spoken to you.

A great way to use this is to help you proofread your writing, whether it is an email, a report, or a page of a book. Having your own words spoken to you can help you identify mistakes or potential improvements.

Bonus Materials

In addition to the 101 tips here, I've put together a few more just-for-fun ones. These are crazy easter eggs hidden in your Mac and other fun stuff. In addition, there is a custom contact form to email me if you have a question about the book. I may add some demonstration videos there, too, if I get enough requests about a particular tip.

To get to the bonus materials section, just go to

http://macmost.com/tips-book-bonus

and register your book. All you need is your email address and the code:

TIPSBOOK88

Made in the USA
Charleston, SC
19 February 2016